Though small, she was a big presence.

For Dinga, my African sister,
and for all of those who, though small, are a big presence;
whose lives, though short, drench the world with color;
whose hearts, though beating irregularly,
effectively and unforgettably teach ours.

Dinga died at the age of fourteen on Wednesday, May 20, 2009,
of a mitral valve prolapse during yet another fight with malaria.

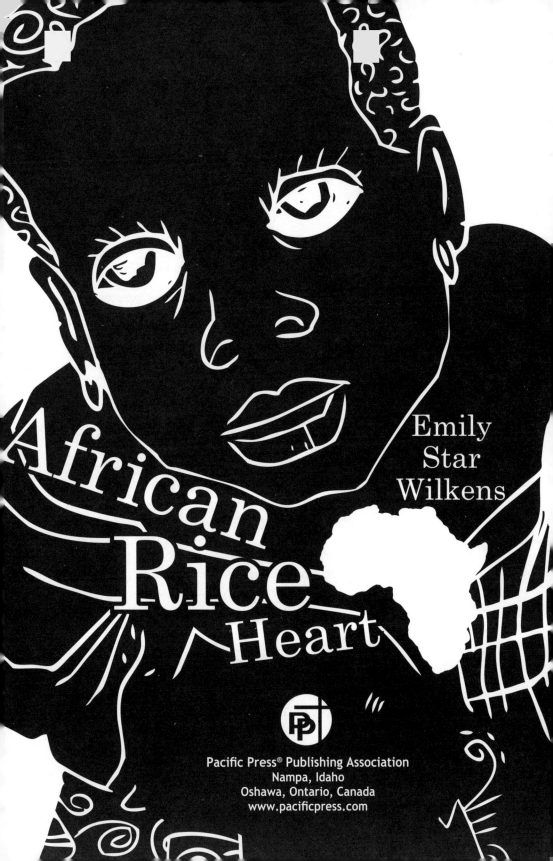

African Rice Heart

Emily
Star
Wilkens

Pacific Press® Publishing Association
Nampa, Idaho
Oshawa, Ontario, Canada
www.pacificpress.com

Cover design by Ben Jepson based on a block print by Emily Star Wilkens
"Special thanks to Professor Brent Bergherm of the Graphic Design Program at Walla Walla
University and the Visual Communications Club for your help with cover design."
Photos supplied by author
Inside design by Steve Lanto

Copyright © 2011 by Pacific Press® Publishing Association
Printed in the United States of America
All rights reserved

The author assumes full responsibility for the accuracy of all facts and quotations as cited in this
book.

Scriptures quoted from NKJV are from The New King James Version, copyright © 1979,
1980, 1982, Thomas Nelson, Inc., Publishers.

Scripture quotations marked NLT are taken from the Holy Bible, New Living Translation,
copyright © 1996, 2004. Used by permission of Tyndale House Publishers, Inc., Wheaton,
Illinois 60189. All rights reserved.

Scripture quotation from The Message. Copyright © by Eugene H. Peterson, 1993, 1994, 1995,
1996, 2000, 2001, 2002. Used by permission of NavPress Publishing Group.

You can obtain additional copies of this book by calling toll-free 1-800-765-6955 or by visiting
http://www.adventistbookcenter.com.

Library of Congress Cataloging-in-Publication Data:

Wilkens, Emily Star, 1986-
African rice heart : a young woman's journal of radical service /
Emily Star Wilkens.
p. cm.
ISBN 13: 978-0-8163-2402-6 (pbk.)
ISBN 10: 0-8163-2402-6 (pbk.)
1. Wilkens, Emily Star, 1986- 2. Missionaries—Chad—Biography.
3. Missionaries—United States—Biography. 4. Nurses—Chad—Biography.
5. Chad—Social conditions. 6. Chad—Social life and customs. I. Title.
BV3625.C48W55 2011
266.0092—dc22

2010054215

11 12 13 14 15 • 5 4 3 2 1

Contents

Part One

African Rice Heart

I remember the first day my African host family *allowed* me to draw water for my morning bucket-shower. Before that day, they did everything for me. They didn't allow me to lift things, to stand, or to do work of any kind. One of the other volunteers told me this was their way of welcoming me and that I would offend them if I insisted too soon that I be treated like everyone else. But their kindness made me feel like a ritzy American sissy, distant and different, so after two weeks I put my foot down and said I'd get the water for my shower myself.

Going to our open-air well, which isn't lined, isn't capped, and isn't treated, I grasped the end of a very dirty rope and tossed a plastic bucket—cracked from hauling heavy loads—down into the greenish liquid. Then, peering down into the well, I waited for the bucket to fill. Instead, stubbornly, it floated. I jerked the rope right and then left, trying to catch the lip of the bucket in the water so it would fill. Eventually, it did catch, but then it submerged completely and came up too full and heavy.

I tried to pull the bucket up like my African siblings do, hand over hand and away from the dirt wall of the well, but it scraped the whole way up, scooping dirt off the wall that then became a brown layer across the water's surface.

Sucking up my fast-diminishing pride, I struggled to keep my knee-length, blue-and-white-striped bathrobe modestly tied shut while I carried the bucket across the courtyard. I leaned far to the right to counter the weight of the water, which was pulling my left arm and shoulder down, and the water sloshed against my calf and ran down my ankle. The people who were watching tried not to laugh. I was embarrassed.

As I entered the outdoor "shower room," my stomach turned at the sight

My African family's shower room made of mud bricks and open to the sky. Unfortunately, it also served as the family's walk-in urinal.

of the yellow puddles and the sweet stench of urine. The shower room was also the site of the activity described by the French verb *pisser*. Bricks were scattered on the ground, and you were supposed to be able to stay *above* whatever was *below* by standing on them. But that smell—no way to avoid it.

I set my bucket in one corner of the mud enclosure and tipped it slightly, washing some of the urine out of the drain hole. Then I did a slow, careful dance across the bricks; draped my towel, bathrobe, and underwear over the wall; and stood there naked, wondering once again just how this shower was going to get me clean.

I'm pretty sure I've never been quite that exposed—and I'm not referring to the literal exposure: the way my body was sandwiched between the open sky and the ever-present dirt, those white birds peering down at me, and the malarial mosquitoes penetrating my personal space and landing on me rudely. No, I'm talking about the exposure to everything unfamiliar in the Chadian culture—everything I couldn't swallow. As I thought about how exposed I was, I peered over the wall and saw Dinga, my fourteen-year-old African sister, pounding rice for the evening meal.

Dinga had a lot of power in her thready biceps. Her wrists flexed as she slammed the pole down to crush the kernels that lay in the wooden bowl. Sometimes, when she'd throw the pole up, she'd let go of it, clap twice to show off her skill, and then catch the pole again—her arms reengaging with surprising force. She was working alone, and she was sweating.

We eat rice at almost every meal. "It brings force," the Chadians say, which I would translate to something more like "it fills our bellies," because white rice really has very little nutritional value. But it means survival nonetheless.

Making the rice edible is a long, hard process—something I'm not used to. My African family's patience with the demands of this lifestyle is admirable. They'll spend all afternoon and part of the evening preparing a meal, and thirty minutes after they set out the food, the children are scraping the crusty rice out of the bottom of the pot.

But the process—yikes! The ground has to be softened, the seeds have to be planted, the rains must come, and the family must tend to the growth. When the green stalks have finished their growth and then browned with death, the people go to the fields to harvest the grain. With their hatchets balanced on their heads, bottles filled with murky water swinging at their sides, and babies sleeping, tied hard against their backs, they—the women—work the fields.

"The women work harder than you men do," I told my lazy African brothers. "Women—they get up early, sweep the courtyard, cook the breakfast, take care of the children, work the rice fields, come home, make dinner, and host guests. They do everything. What do you do?"

David, a lean brother with little ambition, said, "We build the houses."

"That's *one* thing," I replied with a smile.

"Emily, you don't know," David said, defending his gender.

Well, maybe I don't know the whole story. But I do know that the women work hard.

The women, they work those
    fields.
And yes, the men do too.
And the children.
Really, everyone, because this
    is everyone's business.
Food in the belly is everyone's business.

Jolie and I cut rice in her field.

After the stalks are cut, they're tied in bundles and left in the sun to dry for several days. Next, they're hauled to the center of the field, which becomes the threshing floor. There, in what may be the most physically demanding part of the process, the harvesters thresh the rice, slamming the bundles onto the ground with back-breaking effort. They call it "tapping the rice," but really they're beating it—almost as if they're punishing it. This process breaks the sheathed kernels from the stalk. The harvesters sweep the freed rice kernels into piles, load them into basins, and carry them home, where they spread them out on tarps to dry some more and then pound them like Dinga was doing, stripping off the sheaths—the chaff. Sometimes two people, or even three, stand around a bowl throwing the thick wooden pole down on the rice—taking turns and breaks and turns again. Sometimes the pounding will go on for an hour.

Pound.
Heave.
Pass.
Next.
Blister.
Pound.

I've joined them many times, but I know they were just humoring me. I suppose they think it's humor*ous* as well. I'm awkward and unpracticed— I mean, I didn't learn this as a kid. At one break, I showed my sisters the blisters on my hands, and they laughed and called Mama Jolie over. She didn't laugh at me, but instead ran her fingers over the blisters and shook her head back and forth. Those blisters that formed on my callus-free fingers were testaments to the fact that changing the state of the rice is no easy process. And the process *does* greatly change the rice.

When they think they've pounded the rice enough, they lift a bowl filled with chaff and rice kernels high and pour the mixture out, allowing the wind to blow the chaff away while the kernels—the "eyes" of rice—fall into a bowl on the ground. Sometimes, when the air is still, they'll run down the road pouring the rice and chaff from one bowl to another and letting the wind created by their running blow the chaff away. In the evenings, then, you can find thick trails of chaff in the roads alongside the huts.

At this point, they remove the impurities, shaking the eyes of the rice and scanning them carefully.

Get it all out.
All the rocks.
All the sticks.
All the bugs.

After they've gotten rid of the big stuff, they pour the rice into a bowl of water to be washed—gently. Dinga scolds me for rushing this part, for sloshing water all over the place. She washes in a way that is almost artful, and the rocks that may have been missed in the picking stage sink to the bottom of the bowl, and they pour the pure rice off.

At this point, the rice is clean and bare, stripped of all that had covered it. It's ready to be cooked, boiled; the last step—the softening, swelling, sterilizing step. We're plagued by *Giardia* and worms, by typhoid and amoebas. The boiling helps to prevent protruding worm bellies, persistent diarrhea, and feverish suffering.

What a variety of treatments the rice is exposed to! What a trip it goes on from the beginning of its existence to the end! One moment the stalks are being hacked down, and the next someone is picking out all the contaminants. One moment the kernels are being pounded, and the next they're being washed. But after all the pounding, sifting, and washing, the rice swells as it is being boiled. It swells to become something more than what it was, and then we're thankful for each step of the process.

And here in the midst of this sometimes-hell-sometimes-heaven place, I feel like my own heart has gone on a trip—one that has left it exposed.

It's as if someone played soccer with it,
rubbed it against a cheese grater,
gave it a nice warm bath,
threw it a birthday party,
and then made it run a marathon.

Things here in this village and hospital make me feel and think things I've never felt or thought before. I didn't know that welling-up, uncontainable, giggly contentment could get inside me like it has, but then a baby was born into my hands, screaming and pinky-brown. I also didn't know the whirling, gut-tingling, skin-tightening, pinchy-eyed sorrow that humans can feel—until I listened to a baby's silent, still chest through my stethoscope and realized that death was certain.

We can't tell what effect exposure will have on people. Sometimes it seems to strengthen them immediately—the "rising to the challenge" effect. Other times it takes a long while for its effects to show up; and still other times the effects of exposure to life's extremes begin right away and seem never to let up. Many of our *why* questions don't get answered on this earth, which can turn our search for answers into a desperate grasp at peace—something that we'll find only when we set our gaze on Someone and someplace beyond our full comprehension.

When I bump into the walls of our shower room, dirt sticks to my wet skin. It's frustrating. I want my shower to bring equal cleanliness to my whole body, and the fact that my feet never get beyond a light shade of brown bothers me. It isn't comfortable here—there isn't enough sanitation

11

nor enough privacy. But in some ways the very things that make me so uncomfortable also bring me so much comfort.

At night, when I've finished my shift, during which I've become convinced that humankind can't dodge hardships, I come home from the hospital and shower. Sometimes, I dunk my whole head in my bucket and hold it underwater for a few seconds—a silly thing to do, really, but it drowns all sounds, all noises, and something about it makes me feel like I'm sticking my head out the window of a house that's filled with smoke. It's like I'm getting a breath of fresh air.

Once I've gotten my head wet, I pour water over the rest of my body, and those bars of soap that my mom assured me I'd need come in really handy. I just want the odors to come off—the stench of the penicillin that is shot out of cheap syringes and flows into and burns the veins of the woman who, without it, will die of worse; the stench of the sweaty bodies that have gone unbathed for far too long; the odors that trigger the pictures of the patients we left at the shift's end.

> In this African shower room I feel too exposed,
> but there's a part of me that,
> at night,
> when I really need to know there is something greater out there,
> wants nothing more than to be exposed to that night sky and its white
>   lights,
> wants nothing more than the truth to be that the ceiling is high,
> and hope lies *there,* beyond the things seen.

And when I am done showering and still grasping my shampoo bottle, some soft, smoky scent drifts over the low shower wall, and the laugh of some wild child trickles over it too. And I'm thankful for the low walls— for that ceilingless shower.

> We're exposed to the stars *and* the urine.
> The hellish *and* the holy.
> The pleasant *and* the unpleasant.
> The pounding *and* the washing.
> The sifting *and* the boiling.

What you'll read in the following pages is a collage of both.

people are good

Here I am. I'm twenty-two. I'm heading to Chad, Africa, to work for six months at a hospital in the village of Béré. I'll be filling a nursing position, though I'm not a nurse. I'm impulsive, a slight bit disorganized, have a bad memory, a big fear of dogs, a little fear of the dark, and this itch inside me to please people. Those are some of the things our Father in heaven is going to have deal with this year. Sometimes, I wonder if wanting to help is enough. Does willingness really equal usefulness?

Will He turn my weaknesses into strengths?
Will He use me *in* my weakness?
When fear of failing seeps in, will He remind me what courage feels like?
Will I somehow be brave and step up to big, tough, scary tasks?
Will He teach me to turn these anxieties into prayers?
Will He? I'm banking on it.

I said Goodbye to my parents, Joyce and Keith, and to my boyfriend, Alex, at the airport. I'd already said Goodbyes to my brothers and friends, but these last goodbyes seemed harder and more final. My mom reminded me that these were happy goodbyes because I'm beginning such a neat experience, and we'll see each other in no time—we are rather optimistic people! So, instead of crying, we smiled with puddles in our eyes.

My mom sneaked all sorts of things into my bags. I'm finding baby dolls, wooden giraffes, orange purses containing quarters, string, an emergency siren, and a million bars of soap. I never use bar soap at home, but she assured me I'd use it, and she was right.

My mom comes from this line of unique, creative, artistic, slightly wild and yet extremely capable women. She's an actor, a musician, a painter, a wood-carver, a museum docent, a seamstress, and a rock hound. As we were driving on one of our family vacations, my mom screamed, "Stop the car!" She said she'd just seen a beaver on the side of the road, roadkill, and she wanted to get its tail and have a taxidermist stuff it. Then, she said, she'd let the kids at church see a beaver's tail up close, and they could feel it! My dad said, "Joyce—" but knowing how persistent she is, he pulled over to the side of the road and told her there was a hatchet in the trunk. She did actually hack the tail off, sending beaver blubber flying all around. Do you see what I mean?

Yet despite all this seeming eclecticness, Mom's one of the most organized, thorough, and thoughtful people I've ever met. Her love pours itself into service to the people around her, and I felt it as she did everything she could to help me prepare for Africa and to get there.

So many other people did the same—it seems like I've had an army behind me. But as I was getting on that plane, I realized that army couldn't get on the plane with me, so I was going to have to stuff their "good courage" and "best wishes" into my pockets to pull out when I dropped into pits.

My seat was next to Courtney, a makeup artist on her way to Paris. She's created her own lip gloss, and listening to her talk passionately about the colors, ingredients, and effects of her product started me dreaming in a way that hasn't ended yet. People who do what they love are magnetic and inspiring. I want to do a lot of wondering about my career this next year. Sometimes I'm afraid that I'll end up doing what I *should* and I'll miss what *could have been.*

I arrived in Washington, D.C., at three in the afternoon, and when I checked on my flight to Africa, I found that it had been delayed. Instead of leaving at eight thirty that night, it was scheduled to depart at two in the morning. Oh dear! With so much time to kill, I decided to see something of our nation's capital. I asked about the best way to get into the city, and a chatty woman in a crisp airport uniform told me that taxis charge forty dollars one way. Yikers! She recommended that I try to bum a ride on one of the free airport shuttles. *Oooh*—resourceful and thrifty!

I lugged my huge backpack almost half a mile to the H2 station and asked Scotty, the Comfort Inn driver, when the next shuttle would leave for the hotel. He said, "Soon," and asked me what room I was staying in. "Errr . . . ummm," I stammered, "well, I don't exactly have a reservation. Could I please have a ride though? I'd like to leave the airport, but taxis are so expensive."

Scotty said that he had "nice bones in his body," and with that he opened the door and pointed me to the front passenger's seat. While we waited for the van to fill up, Scotty peppered me with questions about my trip. Then, just as we were pulling away, a woman ran up to my window and slipped me a twenty-dollar bill, saying she had heard us talking about where I was going and she wanted to give me the money because "everyone needs help once in a while." PEOPLE are GOOD!

A whole airline crew was riding the shuttle to the hotel, and entertaining conversations soon sprouted. The slightly abrasive yet funny senior pilot asked me where I was going. As I told him what I knew about my destination, he began to give me a stream of reasons why I was crazy, concluding, "You are nuts, girl! There's no way I would ever go there!"

Suddenly, I felt a bit nervous. Had I overlooked the risk? Hadn't I given my decision to go enough thought? Debra, one of the flight attendants, rolled her eyes a bit at the pilot and reassured me. She said I was brave and that I shouldn't listen to what the others were saying. I appreciated what she said so much; she etched her mark inside of me.

I met lots of nice people in D.C., did a variety of things, among them tripping in a crosswalk directly in front of loads of traffic, landing facedown with my huge backpack on top of me. The ground has never come at me so fast. I couldn't do anything but laugh and wave to all the drivers, who, though sympathetic, were impatiently waiting for me to get out of the way.

When I finished wandering D.C., I made my way back to the Comfort Inn, hoping to catch Scotty and ride another shuttle back to the airport. When I asked where he was, though, I was told his shift had ended. Max, who was driving during the evening shift, asked me where I needed to go. I told him I needed to catch a plane, and he said, "All right; I'll take you." I felt bad, though, because I wasn't staying at the hotel and I was going to be the only passenger on the whole ten-person shuttle. So I confessed—I told Max that I wasn't a customer of the hotel. He smiled and said that it was no problem, that he wasn't doing anything anyway, so he'd take me back to the airport. Once again—PEOPLE are GOOD!

I slept through most of my fifteen-hour flight to Africa. But I didn't get to Chad right away—I spent a day and a half delayed in Addis Ababa, Ethiopia. The airline put me up in a hotel and fed me three meals a day of good rice, veggies, eggs, soup, fresh bread, salad, yogurt, and hot cocoa. One morning, two other volunteers and I took a taxi and went all over town.

It's a different world here. That's all I can say for now. I can tell I'm starting to process all these things I'm seeing. I just wrote a paragraph of thoughts that have been going through my mind but found myself "backspacing" them away because they don't make sense. *I* haven't made sense of it yet. People who have traveled to second and third world countries know exactly what I'm talking about and what I'll have to process. What about all these beggars? They're not begging for money or for drugs. These are legitimately needy people who want food. What about all those sad lions we saw at the Addis zoo? They look so unhappy. What about this defensive mode of mine—this feeling that everyone is out to get me in one way or another? Should I have this attitude? Does it make me safe? It doesn't seem to fit with focusing on others rather than on myself.

Sort. Sort. Sort.
File this thought here.
Dismiss that one.
Dwell on this one.
Yes, this one matters.
Oh—this is just the beginning!

we arrive

I've arrived. When we flew to the capital, N'Djamena, and stepped off the plane, a wall of heat hit my body. The desert is trying to suck me dry already, and I found myself sipping at my Nalgene and wiping sweat droplets from my forehead with my wrist before they slid into my eyes.

Levi, a strong, confident Chadian and an employee of the hospital in Béré, was sent to make sure we found our way safely. We trusted him completely because we had no other choice—we don't speak French, and English is rare. We rode in a bus for seven hours. When the bus ride ended, we were greeted by moto drivers who surrounded us and our baggage on all sides. Each begged, saying they'd take us for a "good price" and grabbing our bags before we agreed. Levi handled everything evenly, with a calm that I will thank him for later. I imagine doing this on my own, and then I stop because it's a *baaaaaaad* thought. Finally, Levi agrees with certain drivers on a fair price, and our bags were bungeed down two high behind us on the mopeds. For the rest of our trip, we were wheeling down roads that looked like lakes—we are arriving at the end of the short wet season. After I surrendered the idea of death by moto wreck and decided to trust my driver, everything became more fun. I said to myself awfully naively, "I don't want this ever to end!"

Ansley Howe was on the moto in front of me. Ansley is an extremely brave twenty-four-year-old nurse from Maryland. She's of medium height and has brown curls that love this humid atmosphere. Our fathers went to medical school together, but while those ties already exist, they'll be cinched down this next year. I know she'll be my shoulder, and I'll try to be hers.

Ansley's moto driver seemed to be stopping to drink something from a small bottle that he kept in a brown paper sack. With one waft, Ansley knew her driver was drinking a fairly strong intoxicant and coupling it with driving; and while we laughed a bit at the new set of rules (or perhaps just the abandonment of all the ones we are used to), it also made us nervous.

And there were wrecks. Numerous ones left Ansley and me knee-deep in water with our skirts hiked up "hilltops," in complete disregard of the no-knees-showing cultural faux pas. Our bags, by some grace (not granted by our drivers), stayed relatively dry.

At one point well after nightfall, we stopped briefly. When I looked down at the monster puddles in our trail, I saw that the stars were bouncing their reflections off the water, leaving white dots on the surface. Though it may sound clichéd, it was perfect.

My bum hurt wickedly as we neared our destination, and I was no longer wishing for a never-ending moto ride. All of my anticipatory nerves had wilted in those three hours; but as we arrived at the seventy-bed hospital in the village of Béré, those nerves were once again livened.

Two young men, volunteers as well, unloaded my bags, and I followed them as they dragged the bags down a dusty road and turned left into a cluster of huts. Even though it was past their bedtime, an uncountable number of quiet African children greeted me with timid stares. But their shyness was OK for now—we don't share a language yet. A quiet woman led me to my hut and swung the tin door open for me, and I walked into the empty, dark space. The interior smelled like a musky greenhouse—that combo of hot air and wet dirt. A cot sat against one wall, and a white mosquito net haphazardly flopped in a pile at its foot—*and that was it!* And in a way—well actually, not just one way, but in most ways—I'm happy that I've been given such a bare beginning.

"Emptiness is a good conductor," my good friend Trina told me that when I was at a really low point—feeling like all life had been dumped out of me. I've been carved and defined by a busy life, like most American twentysomethings—a life densely populated by required experiences, appointments, college years, extracurriculars, and stuff, good and bad, that *just happens.* And it all shapes us. It's been a life that many people might call cluttered, and sometimes I think I do a lot of *RE-acting* to whatever comes my way instead of *acting* and choosing it for myself. I don't think it's *all* clutter, but yes, life can become so busy that those THINGS and EXPERIENCES choose who you become. So this emptiness was a new side to things.

Emptiness is the most intentional conductor.
Clean canvases make the most original paintings.
And pure, straight-up water is the best thing for you anyway.

I was tired that night, and without any socialization, eating, or setting up of camp, I fell asleep on my cot, curled up in a ball. Now, as I'm writing this here in the morning, my ankles and feet, which were uncovered during the night, are peppered with mosquito bites. I'm nervous about what will fill this emptiness—nervous, with a grand attempt at courage.

first evening

It's my first full evening in my new home, and I'm crying already. I'm usually not much of a crier, but tonight, I can't plug my eyes.

As dusk settled in, they put me in my dark mud hut to eat alone. Supposedly, it's a real honor to get to eat like this—to have your own bowl of food and not be "disturbed" by the joyous noise of happy children. They definitely don't know me yet.

The food is so unfamiliar. It's a huge ball of rice, resembling half of a volleyball. The rice is called *boule* (pronounced like *pool* but with a *b*). No one told me how to eat this. I started by using a fork to cut off chucks of this rice ball and chewing them down. Then, about halfway through the meal, I discovered a sauce in a tiny pot. When I tasted it, I could tell it was fish in a slimy liquid. Feeling queasy, I continued eating the rice plain.

They won't let me do a thing for myself. When I walk out of my hut, three sweet Africans, young and old alike, get up off of whatever they're sitting on and run it over to me. If I'm carrying something, five people come to relieve me. It's just overwhelming.

Oh, and then there's my French. I can't say anything except "thank you." I'm rarely understood. Even when I try seven different pronunciations of the letters in the English-French dictionary and use different tones and volumes coupled with hand motions and sound effects, all I get back are blank stares and *fake* nods of understanding.

It seems I'm in this glass room all by myself. I see everything that's going on around me, but my eyes are the only sense of any use these days. These ears should come with translators.

family

We are nineteen in all. We're eclectic, eccentric, hectic, spastic, and mystic. Yes, mystic. I will live with this family for the next six months. I'm paying them sixty dollars a month to rent a mud hut and to eat two meals a day with them. The ones who are educated—the men and the older children—speak French. But the younger ones and Jolie, the mother, speak in a quirky dialect called Nangjere. Some of the words sound like *"booja,"* *"tumalung,"* *"di di,"* and *"oh oh."* I stifle my laughs because I have no way to explain what I think is funny, but it's hard to take the words seriously!

I said we are mystic. I say that because I've realized there is this special mystery of family dynamics that is uniquely gifted to each family across the world. I've known lots of types of families: Families who raise their children out in the countryside and don't eat salt or mustard. Families who raise their babies in cars and who travel to foreign countries, carrying their children with them in backpacks. Families who go to high church and dress their children in matching sweaters. Families with one parent. Families who yell. And families who never really talk. The family I'm staying with has some mystery of its own, like nothing I've seen before, and I'm intrigued.

Jolie, me, and Samedi, who Jolie says—with pride—is big now.

Chadian families are big for a number of reasons. They have yet to use birth control regularly, and family planning just doesn't happen. And in a country that is so dependent on the rice they grow for themselves, the more children they have, the larger the rice field they can maintain.

But this family isn't big for either of those reasons. Samedi and Jolie, the father and mother, have an advanced case of bigheartedness, and it has resulted in nineteen family members. Among them, besides their children, their children's spouses, and their grandchildren, they've taken on, adopted, four others. What a family! Eclectic, eccentric, hectic, spastic, and mystic.

Samedi and Jolie married young—when he was eighteen, and she was fifteen. Jolie told me she was *"verrrrrrrrry"* skinny back then. They were newlyweds, and money for food didn't come easily.

Here in Africa, being skinny means you're unloved, and conversely, if you carry weight, it's because someone loves you and spends money to put food in your belly. Sometimes, even love isn't enough to make you fat, though, and Jolie and Samedi felt the pinch in their younger years. Jolie tells me Samedi is big now. She says it with pride because she loves him so much.

the sea of the sick

The hospital's seventy beds are filled and emptied in a tidal-like flow—it's the sea of the sick. Someone is admitted at midnight and then another discharged in the morning, so another can take his place. In and out; they come and go. The hospital is always dynamic during the day—doctors improvising tactics and treatments; nurses taking notes and changing dressings, starting and restarting IVs, and scolding patients for charging their phones on the precious solar power that will last only till midnight and then all will go black. At night the hospital becomes a quieter place where family members or caretakers curl up under the beds of their sick, sleeping on concrete—illegally. Families are supposed to camp outside and leave the aisles between the beds open so the nurses can give midnight meds. But no one likes the mosquitoes, and so the healthy sneak into the sea of the sick.

Only two or three nurses work during the eighteen-hour night shifts, so the families are responsible for feeding, bathing, and walking the sick to the restrooms, which are out back and crawling with cockroaches. The nurses are responsible for changing dressings, injecting insulin, giving meds, and monitoring post-surgery patients, maternity patients, and those who are critically ill.

There is a cooking shelter where women boil water, prepare rice, and cook the meat that they will feed their sick. Yesterday, a woman asked me to try her soup. Fortunately, I'm not proficient enough in the language to ask her what was in it and just gave my nodding approval after downing the chunky liquid. If I were to know what was in it, I might not approve!

When patients arrive at the hospital, they give their small yellow *carne*—the Chadian medical record book—to the nurse and then take a seat on the skinny cement benches in front of the emergency room. They arrive early to avoid the heat that comes despite the speckled shadows under the mango tree leaves. When their names are called, their vitals will be taken. The glass thermometer is pulled out of a makeshift holder, a cylindrical plastic cup containing bleach and cotton balls that have probably been in there for days "cleansing" the thermometer after it has taken hundreds of axillary and rectal temperatures. Next, the pulse is found in the wrist, the breathing is observed and recorded, and then the cuff is strapped onto their skinny arms, and their blood pressure is measured.

Following this taking of their vitals, the patients will pay to have a consultation, during which their liver and stomach are palpated and they are asked many questions. How long have you had diarrhea? How many times a day? How many times have you vomited? Do you have a fever? How many weeks has this leg been infected? How long has the piece of metal been in your foot? When did the hippo attack you? Things like that. The potential illnesses are determined, and the nurse orders lab tests. Pee in a cup. Stool sample—collected in a mango leaf. Finger prick—checking hemoglobin levels and malarial concentrations. Lumbar puncture—checking for meningitis. If the case is dire, requiring hospitalization, the patient is given one of the five emergency-room beds and perhaps an IV may be started—fluids are often given. If the case isn't pressing, then the lab tests are done and the patient waits outside on one of those skinny benches until the results come back—which could take all day.

When the lab results come back for those waiting on the skinny benches, their names are called and they are told the suggested treatment. If it's malaria—quinine. If the test for malaria has a negative result, the patient is still told to take quinine because the lab test is so inaccurate— it's simply a microscopic observance of malarial cells. If the lab reports worms—PZQ and mebendazole. If it's something worse, like meningitis or tetanus—hospitalization and aggressive treatments to save the patient from those mean diseases. A nurse—one nurse—sees and treats more than fifty patients a day in the outpatient clinic.

The pediatrics ward holds babies on adult-sized beds. The mothers often sleep on the bed next to their child. Sometimes, babies cry all night, and the air is stuffy in the small ward. Long sticks are tied to the corners of each bed, and at night, the mothers tie mosquito nets to them. The families are asked to keep their child's area clean, to sweep it and clean up spilled food or other messes. It's a small place for so many to try to get well.

The medical-surgery ward is bigger. A cement wall divided it into two rooms—the men's ward and women's, giving a slight bit of privacy since the beds lie side by side with not even a curtain in-between. The patients know each other's business—know their neighbor's health and could probably tell the doctor more about the number of times they threw up or how much water they drank during that day than the nurse on duty could. Patients share water with each other, and their children play together to pass long days in that bad environment. Sickness brings them together—especially chronic sickness and its demand for long stays at the hospital.

The delivery room is small and gets crowded when too many people try to help deliver the baby. There is a metal bed in one corner of the room that is wrapped with a vinyl sort of covering. This is quite convenient because after the placenta has been fully delivered and the mother moved to a more "comfortable" place in the maternity ward, the metal bed can be drenched in bleach water in an attempt to sterilize the room for the next birth. The maternity ward is available for mothers and babies who need to recover after difficult deliveries, C-sections, or other complications.

Preemie baby: screaming, hollering—and alive!

Dr. James Appel and his operating-room team do surgeries during the day and at night in the case of emergencies. The operating room is as close to sterile as possible—and when a fly starts buzzing around the overhead lights, measures are taken to get it out. The equipment is old, but the surgeries done amaze me.

At the exit, John Jac, the gate guard, sits smiling in his green army shirt. He keeps the creaky metal gate locked, regulating the tidal flow. And when one patient gets well, he opens the gate and lets him or her flow on out—out to be well in the world again, to go back to living again.

Part Two

Huts

The sky spreads out big here. It has that Montana, Texas, or Nebraska feel—where the "flatitude" makes you see more sky than you do land, so you find yourself believing that it actually IS bigger.

The end of the rainy season has been so green and wet. I'm supposed to enjoy the change because supposedly it's not going to last long. In the first weeks, we have taken some walks to the river, which is about four miles away. Our walks were more like treks through marshlands—like walking through mashed potatoes or something. I kept losing my sandals in the mud and gave up wearing them after a while. Nathaniel, a Danish volunteer, did too and acquired worms—they got him real sick. Apparently, you can get them right up through your feet.

The huts here are similar to gingerbread houses—just as a really good gingerbread house is made only of edible materials, so, too, many of these huts are fashioned entirely of natural things: mud bricks (made from soil, water, sand, and some vegetation), branches for trusses, grass ties around the trusses, grass roofs, and dirt floors. You could smash a hut down and not leave a bit of garbage. As eco-friendly as it is, when the rainy season comes,

Outdoor living quarters, where we cook, eat, sleep, and socialize.

23

houses are easily damaged—mud walls just disintegrate, and people have to do a lot of rebuilding when the rains stop.

storm

Sometimes nature seems so violent, and African weather is a stranger to me—unfamiliar and intimidating. Last night at about 10 P.M., I was awake in my hut, sitting in the dark, on the edge of my cot, a bit paralyzed as I listened to the rain crash on my upscale tin roof. The rain fell so hard that the pitters and patters weren't even distinguishable. It was more like those drummers who hammer the cymbals with both drumsticks at once and crease their faces in violent ways while they do. Anyway, that's how it made me feel. I imagined the rest of the family all huddled together in their huts in good company, and then me, lonely and scared. I wanted to be with them, but though being alone was scary, I was also scared of going out there in the dark storm and scared of what the family would think when I asked to come in to their hut. When I write it out, I can see that's a whole lot of fear, and in hindsight, I want to say, Suck it up, Emily.

All of a sudden a woman was yelling and banging on my door. Could this night get any scarier? I cracked my door open, and as soon as I did, a wall of wind-driven water hit me. The woman, frantic and extremely drunk, began yelling things over the extremely loud rain, but I could barely hear her and definitely couldn't understand any of what she was saying—I've only been here a week, and my French is really awful and/or nonexistent. But as we stood there under my door frame, I could "hear" with my eyes that she was worried about her baby, who was strapped to her back and tightly covered in fabric. She wanted help or money, I wasn't sure which.

I was scared and uncertain about what I should do, so since I live right next to the hospital, I told her seriously and rather shortly to go over there—that there were nurses there who could help her. She shook her head, said something more in French, waited for my response, and then in frustration ran off in the rain with her umbrella pulled tightly down over her body.

I moved out of the rain, closed my door hard against the wind, and just stood there, unable to digest that weird situation and my reaction and feelings. Not knowing if I had done the right thing, a million questions flew into my mind.

How did she know where I lived?

Was the baby really sick?

Was it an emergency?

Why was she so panicked?

Should I have at least brought her into my hut, out of the rain?

Maybe she really didn't have any money and that's why she didn't go to the hospital?

I decided that I was disappointed at how I had reacted. Even if I *had* done the right thing, I had acted completely out of fear and panic.

Running my hands over my drenched clothes, I realized that not only were they wet, but they were also caked in mud. As I pulled them off of me, I realized that the rain that had been hitting the dirt walls of my hut had been throwing mud all over me! I climbed into bed and pulled my dry sheets around my damp body. My mind continued to race through the interaction, and I continued to feel frustrated with my actions. But eventually, when my mind was tired of running, I slipped into sleep.

With the morning came clearer thinking. I wished my reaction could have been more loving and less fear motivated. I wished I would have done things differently. I wished I knew more French. I wished I was more compassionate. But this morning I realize that this is something that I'm going to have to work at; that I'm going to have to allow myself to learn. I tend to kick myself for not acting *this way*, not doing *that* just a little bit differently, not being a better friend, sister, or daughter. But kicking ourselves just leaves us all beat up. We're mistake-makers. We're imperfect. Learning and then letting go is hard but necessary. Bounce back. Attempt. Pray. Fail. Learn. Try again. I can tell there will be a lot of that.

and they fed me beans

I'm not a picky eater. Sometimes, I'd take two minutes to prepare my meal while my brothers, who sandwich me in age, would take forty-five minutes, preparing gourmet pizzas and plum tortes. Give me a whole tomato and two bananas along with a tortilla and I'm set. I'll eat them all separately, they'll all go to my stomach, and that will be that. When I'm in a rush, I can grab a carrot or microwave a piece of bread and be on my way.

Many have pitied my future husband, but my dad tells me, "When the student is ready, the teacher will arrive"—that when I need to know how to cook, the desire will come and I'll learn and enjoy it. But for now, there are so many other things that I'd rather be doing.

People's speculations about what I'd be eating here in Chad never worried me. I figured I'd have no problem with whatever they put in front of me. But they eat fish here—a lot of fish.

I've never been able to stomach fish.

I grew up a vegetarian, eating imitation hot dogs and "Fri Chik"—firm brown food that has nothing in common with real chicken. My exposure to meat consisted of childhood visits to my grandparents' house. Every Thanksgiving my grandpa would carve a turkey, but that never seemed like meat to me; it seemed more like "that Thanksgiving dish" because that's the only time we ever had it. Grandma fed us tuna sandwiches more frequently. But if I remember correctly, I ate them with something like enjoyment, connecting them with Grandma—and never with slimy, swimming creatures. So while I'm not allergic to meat, it hasn't been part of my main diet—ever.

I didn't even think I would be such a sissy about this—but I know where the fish they're eating here are coming from. Caught in the local river, they're dehydrated in the sun and the small amount of meat left clinging to spindly bones gets packaged in thin plastic bags and hung in the market. Each fish resembles a gray version of a dried mango. Seriously.

And the meat aisle of the market isn't filled solely with fish. Dangling down from the rafters of the thatch-roofed shops are other grotesque (in my opinion) animals—skinned, filleted, and moist. I almost gag every time I walk through the meat section. Flies march around on the bloody surfaces, and I cringe to think I might have to eat what their feet have touched.

The fish are usually prepared in slimy sauces—ones that you can suck down if your stomach is strong, but I can't do that. I know it. So after being served a slimy fish sauce for my first meal and fearing the newly discovered weakness of my stomach, I asked Sarah, a Danish nurse who has been living here for almost six years, if she could come and tell my family something—maybe that I'm allergic to fish or that they make me a mean person. Or maybe that they make me cry. I didn't care what reason she gave them; I had discovered one of my limits—I can't handle slimy fish sauce.

Sarah agreed, and my family was happy to oblige me. Then they asked me what I liked to eat. I knew beans were cheap, so I told them that I loved beans—and from that time on, I was served beans for every meal—beans soaked in oil and sprinkled with sugar. Breakfast. Dinner. Breakfast. Dinner.

For the first four meals, I was OK with it. Then I started being less excited about mealtimes, and my stomach started feeling sick whenever I saw beans.

One day a while into my new bean diet, I put forth great effort and downed a few bites of the morning meal. But then I set my spoon down and told two big lies: "Thank you, that was delicious," and "I'm *veeerrrryyyy* full now."

Sabine, who speaks her mind and never gives me any breaks, exclaimed, "Eat all your food, Emily!"

Still not knowing much French at all, I pieced together a sentence that conveyed my feelings at that moment. I told her, "Lots of beans. My stomach is mean."

"Turning" the rice to make the evening boule.

She burst out in laughter and took my plate from me. *"Mon vantre est méchant,"* she said, mimicking me in a very high-pitched, wimpy voice, and then she ran to spread the joke to the rest of the family. Since then I haven't seen beans even once. I tried to tell them that beans were fine . . . just not for so many meals in a row! But all they do is say in a mocking tone, "Your stomach will be mean, Emily!" They must think I'm an awfully picky eater.

nice to meet you, death

Before I went to Africa, the only person I'd ever seen take her last breath was Granny, my great-grandma. She was someone extremely unique—she had been a snake charmer and the sword-box lady in the circus, smuggled a baby into America, sold chickens for a living, became a beautician, and danced to my brother's fiddle music even into her nineties.

She died old—ninety-six years old. When we got the call that she wasn't doing well, my mom and I went down to her group home and met my auntie and great-aunt there. Granny's last breaths were far apart, with big spans of nothing in between. Each time she'd exhale, I'd carefully watch to see if her chest would rise again. Her breaths were rattling, unsettling, and unnerving, but that was better than the sound of nothing that came between those breaths.

That sound of nothing is so unnatural for human beings. Even when they try to be as quiet as possible, there's breathing, coughing, fidgeting, and just the general sound of life.

When my granny took her last breath and her chest didn't rise again, my great-auntie's cries for her mama to breath ended the silence. When life ends, we clutch at it. Granny had been so funny, so lively, and now she existed in *memory only*. That experience produced such different emotions than any other I'd experienced.

I knew that when I came to Chad, I'd experience death up close—but I didn't know what that would mean. Granny wasn't in pain when she died, and she was old and I could justify death in that circumstance, saying, "This is part of life, and Granny lived an amazing life." But death in Chad was different.

The small baby girl wasn't even crying anymore when her parents brought in her limp body, and starting an IV line in those bloodless veins felt impossible. I held a flashlight for the Chadian nurse Augustan. He worked calmly, but I felt his urgency—when he missed the vein, he would shake his head in frustration. The bugs swarmed around my flashlight, and their lack of respect in this situation was irritating. I realized they were bugs, but they offended me nonetheless. Nothing about the situation felt good, and when the baby's labored breaths stopped, it felt even worse. I pressed the stethoscope to her tender chest and heard nothing—like the silence at Granny's death. I didn't know what to do with my feelings—they were different from those I felt when Granny died because this was a baby—this was a *beginning,* and it was ending so soon.

In Africa, with its large population, death—even the death of a baby—is an expected and accepted part of life. When in the States our medical staff would be pounding the baby's chest, pushing oxygen into the airways, and administering adrenaline, the African family simply covers her with faded fabric and carries her out, where the weeping will begin. It isn't that people don't fight for life here, but death's arrival is expected—so many families have lost children.

The gut-wrenching feeling I experienced when this baby died would become familiar during my time in Chad. But whether unfortunately or necessarily, I would come to package, to wall off to a fair degree, my reactions to and feelings about death in an urgent attempt to *stay strong*.

And as you would meet an unapologetic killer, I met death for the first time in Africa, with absolutely no pleasure. Nice to meet you, Death? No, it's not nice at all.

everything is

Life is so hard in Africa. Everything takes a long time, and everything makes you sick. Everything is dirty, and everything is scarce. Everything is ancient, and nothing is durable. Everything takes everything. Yet, though everything they have seems like nothing, some invisible thing keeps their spirits high. And to say nothing is good here is to say something that isn't true. These first few days my eyes have been taking it all in, but my observations aren't enough. There's a lot I can't understand.

running

This afternoon I went for a run through the village. Africans don't run very much—in fact, every time *I* run, the adults track me with their eyes like I'm crazy. Many ask me where I'm going. It's like they think I'm moving so fast because I'm going to some important event or on some urgent errand. But I've learned to just say the word *l'exercice*. When I do, they give me a long *"ohhhhhhhhhh"* because, while they probably have never exercised on purpose, the concept is vaguely familiar. The kids though—the kids are a different story. It's a game to them. Some are scared to death of me but can't help but follow. Others are bolder and grab my hands to make sure they keep up.

When I stopped under the mango tree to catch my breath and get out of the sun for a while, I asked the kids if they were tired. "No!" they said. And more children gathered around. I asked the new arrivals if they would like to exercise too. "Yes!" they said. And so, more six-, seven-, eight-, and nine-year-olds joined the group. We jogged farther. We stopped again. More children gathered. More children wanted to exercise. Soon there were more than twenty-five runners. One of the girls at the front of our pack had her baby sister strapped and bobbing on her back.

I watched the adults watch us. Their confused looks made me laugh, and I'd shout out that word *l'exercice* but the group was so large that it was obvious we were no longer strictly about exercise, we were just having fun. And it was *so* fun—so fun that when my body was too tired to go on, my mind was still telling me, *Run!* Finally though, we quit and the children walked off in all different directions to return to whatever they had been doing. Their voices and heavy breathing faded, but the full feeling—the satisfied feeling—that they'd fed me stayed with me as I walked home to shower.

adjustment

In my hut, the invisible heat molecules seem to multiply like the malaria that was recently proven by lab tests to be at significant and increasing levels in my body. The later in the day, the more suffocating my hut becomes. When I move around in there, I keep thinking that I'm going to break into a cool section. But there is no relief with*in*—and barely any in the *out*.

At night, I'd like to prop my tin window open with the little metal rod, but Samedi insists that it's not safe. He very concernedly says, *"Fermez la fenêtre!"* (Close the window!) He's protective and fatherly—taking seriously the idea that I'm his daughter. He's even stricter than my real dad back home.

So I lie in my bed, sweat soaking through my shirt and sheet. I feel like I'm sticking to my cot. I can turn on my side and get some momentary relief, but the new surfaces I'm touching will soon be as hot as those I just left. Sweat. Shirt. Sheet. Stickiness. It's hard to fall asleep, even when you're exhausted.

And I hear this constant beeping. It's clear and comes at regular intervals and I can't pin it down to any one place. My first night in Béré I searched my bags completely through, emptying the contents onto my dirt floor, thinking my alarm clock was going off in one of them. Not finding it, I gave up, shoved orange plugs into my ears, and finally fell asleep. The next morning I imitated the sound for my family and did charades to communicate that the sounds were keeping me awake at night. Then I did the old palms-facing-up quizzical look, asking them to explain where it was coming from. (I'm getting really good at charades.) They drew a bug in the dirt, and I understood.

But that heat. Oh that heat! Please body, adjust quickly. Emily, adjust quickly.

mama pretty

Jolie means "pretty" in French. And she is—with laugh lines that divide her pretty face into pretty sections. Jolie loves on me like I'm her real daughter.

She does the same things that my mom at home does—tucking blankets around my feet, giving me her snacks, and in the case of a headache, pressing her palms on either side of my head to put pressure on my skull. Such commonalities!

Jolie will tease me about things and then take my hand and say, *"Emm-mmillliooo!"* She'll introduce me to her friends and feed me out of her big salad bucket at the market. She worries when my clothes are getting dirty and gives me the fullest cup of tea at tea parties. She sings a song when I come home. It goes, *"Emilio, Emilio tum-ma-lung buja-ooooo!"* which means "Emilio, Emilio, is so hungry!" She tells me she'll send up balloons at my wedding someday; she'll send them up in Africa while I'm getting married in America. She says I must call before I get married. Jolie, your heart is so pretty.

birth

A mother is recovering from a birth in bed 4. It was a C-section, and the baby died. The mother is holding another baby, one who isn't more than a year old. The baby is way too skinny. I brought a cup filled with peanut butter for the baby to eat, but I'm pretty sure the mother ate most of it—everyone is hungry.

Yesterday I took the baby from his tired mother's lap and attached him to my back, carrying him as I gave the noon-day meds. I attached him to my body with a piece of cloth, and while I carried him, he tied his own knots on my heartstrings as he slept there peacefully. He's so small and has gotten such a rough start.

The other patients asked me whose baby I was carrying, and I said, "Mine." Eruptions of laughter shook their bodies, and I worried they would burst their sutures open.

Jolie and her friends tell me that I am too old *not* to have had children. I say, "Please, I'm only twenty-two!" They say it's not normal. But I explain that what's normal for them is highly abnormal where I come from.

I tease my sister Esther, who's sixteen, by asking if she is going to have a baby soon. She laughs and says, "Yes, of course." I know she is only playing along because many African youth, including Esther, dream of getting an education and having smaller families.

Jolie told me that she delivered most of her children completely by herself. No one was home when the contractions began. She showed me how she pulled the babies right out from between her legs, from some sitting position. I put both hands on my head and shook it from side to side because I can't imagine doing that!

Jolie told me she delivered most of her children by herself. No one else was home.

I told her I would yell and scream if I were to give birth to a baby. She said, "No, no, no. That is not good."

What? Not good? I would be having a baby! While I know that it's a very natural thing to have a baby, it just seems like such a supernatural thing at the same time—for your abdomen to be stretched in that way, and the child to grow in there, and then, at birth, move through some canal that will then spit the baby out into cold air. Painful!

Jolie said very seriously that if a woman cries out when she has a baby, someone should hit her. "A woman giving birth should be quiet because that is what is proper."

I asked Jolie if she would hit Esther if she cried just a little when giving birth. Smirking, Jolie said Yes and then let the smirk become a laugh. "Well, I'm going to *sccccrrrreeeeaaamm* loud when I have a baby," I told Jolie. These people are so tough.

The other day we were waiting for a preemie baby to be born and taking guesses on how big it would be, when all of a sudden, the baby came shooting out and lay right there on the table. I grabbed it and took it over to the place where we would clean it up. (It was already screaming loudly.) The mother hadn't made a sound when she delivered the baby, which, I think, is a false representation of just how painful childbirth is.

But someday down the road, having my own baby will be a pinnacle experience—probably magical, and no doubt wonderful. The attachment I've formed while merely carrying someone else's child around on my back for a few hours can't be compared to the true mother-child bond. Give me time though, Jolie. Give me time.

break the rut or break my bones

I love swimming in my skin.

Just my skin.

Maybe some of you are thinking, *OK, Emily, too much information.* But I can't explain to you my full circle of feelings without you understanding today's liberating, skinny-dipping release—exactly what I needed.

I have been feeling anxious and discontent lately. Maybe it's because Nathaniel left yesterday. He was a volunteer from Denmark but because he had dated an American girl for quite some number of years, he was able to speak excellent English with those of us from America, using words like "reconciliation"—impressive! However, once in a while, his choice of words is quite creative—like the time he told me he was "devastated" after running four miles—I think he meant "exhausted."

Since he left, I keep thinking about that reflection phase that he is in— feeling a little jealous even and thinking the grass is thicker and greener where he is. Or maybe I'm simply discontent because I've been feeling weak and sick lately.

I know the hospital has worn on me. The hospital smells especially of disease lately (it's amazing how one infected foot can permeate a whole ward) and the babies' ward is absolutely full—full of sad cases, a few of which, while I try to be optimistic, I'm finding myself being realistic or even pessimistic and that can be really discouraging.

I've talked to my parents a couple times this week because of Thanksgiving and it gets me wishing I was there with them. All of these things just seem to have whirlpooled, forming this giant hole of discontentment. And I've toppled into it.

This morning, Ansley and I woke up (we had a sleepover in my hut) and decided to go to the river. I wanted to run—she wanted to gallop the horses. She's convincing and said Libby, the horse she purchased from the Arabs, needed exercise. Soon we were straddling skinny horses and marching them out the front gate.

My dad loves horses—in fact, when my brothers and I were a lot younger, my family boarded Camp Mivoden's horses through the winter and into the spring. And so I've got funny horse memories from my childhood—like brushing their bellies with weird wire brushes, feeding them corn husks, and riding behind my dad's saddle in the Spokane parade (I was five and wet my pants right onto the bare back of the horse). Quite a few of the memories involve people falling off though and so here in Chad, I've been a bit timid to ride—that blasted fear!

But we cantered through the fields (edging at my comfort level) and then took breaks to let the horses walk, knowing that their undernourished bodies are only equipped with little musclettes and hardly any endurance. I emptied my mind onto the Sahara desert floor and into Ansley's ears, which I'd needed to do—badly.

We tied the bony horses up, pulled off our shoes, and crashed into the filthy water. After being in for a bit, someone said, "Why do we need these swimming suits? We're in the literal, dead, dry, lonely center of Africa!"

With that we stripped down to skin and dove in. It felt riskier than swimming in our suits—like the diseases were more likely to get us.

My grandma was the one who taught me to skinny-dip. She might be a bit embarrassed that I'm writing this, but I'm in Africa, so she can scold me later. Ever since I was young, we'd skinny-dip at Priest Lake. My grandma liked the diving board and I learned to, too. We'd do pencil and swan dives and I learned to do flips eventually too. But the dark water was always looming and there was a bit of surrender that took place there, right before we dove in—a bit of admitting that you didn't know for sure that when the steelhead salmon saw your flashy white skin against the dark water, that they wouldn't come and nibble or chomp at you. The imagination is quite creative. But we'd dive in anyway. There is JUST SOMETHING ABOUT IT.

I remember one time when I was maybe fifteen and my grandma and I were diving, when we noticed a boat with its green navigation light moving in our direction. The boat was getting closer and closer and while I had whipped my suit back on while under the curtain of water, my grandma's suit got caught on her foot and twisted, taking up time she didn't have! Not getting it on in time, we hid in the shadows of our dock while the boat pulled into the dock of our neighbors. My grandma was holding her finger pressed tight to her lips, shushing that pressurized smile on my face—the one that was so close to being laughter. Finally, the people on the boat left and went up to their cabin, and we wrapped up in our big beach towels. There's nothing like that feeling—risky, wild, liberated, and bold.

As I pulled my clothes back on at the African river's edge, I thought, *Sometimes you have to just break the spiraling feeling of discontentment.* You have to do something to remind you that, yes in fact, you are *present* in a place that requires your attention and energy and appreciation. I get frustrated with myself that at times I'm apathetic and even unappreciative of my time here. It happens to me at college and at home too; that rut that has to be broken. And broken it was.

Just as we got our clothes back on, an Arab cow herder walked over the river's bluff. He was beckoning his forty massively horned cows (this is my new fear—I'm not afraid of dogs anymore) to come and drink at the water's edge. It was classic and I felt like we were exotic and invincible—the Saharan desert, the cattle herd following Arab calls, and galloping horses, and us there—exotic. We got back onto our horses and sloppily swung our legs up over the saddles. My hair dripped down my dry shirt and reminded me the whole way home of where I'd just been.

Galloping back, the wind felt like it was pouring through my clothes, in my nose and sucking up my hair into little invisible vacuums or maybe they were knot-making machines. Whatever the case—I achieved wild hair. We RAN those horses home. I kept thinking, *Don't break a bone, Emily, don't break a bone.*

But as I surrendered to that fear, I could tell I was starting to trust the horse, galloping through the rice stalks and passed the huts! I kind of even liked it when the horse would clear his nose and the spray would hit my bare legs. Maybe you would have to experience that to see exactly what I mean.

one of the brothers

Mounden makes me want to put my hand over my heart. It's what I feel like doing when I feel real love for someone.

He's fifteen—he thinks; he doesn't know for sure. None of the kids knows for sure the exact date when they were born because no one keeps track. So, no one celebrates birthdays. Their parents should write these things down, but when you have ten or more kids, it gets hard to remember.

But back to Mounden. When Jolie tells him that he can't eat if he doesn't bathe, he chooses not to eat. Our family teases him mercilessly about his hygiene, saying, "Mounden doesn't bathe," and then we pull up his dirty pant legs to show his dirty calves and feet. Everyone laughs and he smiles and spouts arguments in his defense, "No! No! I bathe!" And he says to Jolie, the ringleader of these attacks, "Mama, you lie!"

Mounden has urinated in the corner of the hut two nights in a row. It's cold during the nights now, and I think he just didn't want to go outside, so he peed in the corner and just let the urine soak into the dirt floor. That did not go over well the next morning. Jolie (mother Africa) was really disgusted and angry, glaring at Mounden and waving her finger in front of his nose.

When I came home last night, no one was there except Jolie and Mounden. We were sitting on a mat all together when Jolie got a phone call and took our lantern with her when she went to answer it. That left Mounden and me sitting in the dark. We talked for a while and then I said, "Mounden, let's have a tea party!" His white teeth flashed even though it was dark, and we both got really excited. I found some lemonade mix, and Mounden got the coal fire going. Then we made our extra-strong-and-sugary lemon tea. Everything about the tea party was genuine.

While we were enjoying our tea, I asked Mounden about his past. He was born into a very poor family. One day, he, his sister, and his mother came through our village of Béré. Jolie saw the mother with her two crying children and asked her where she was going. The woman said she was there to find food because she had none back at home. Jolie told me later that Mounden was extremely skinny and malnourished. Jolie brought a big bowl of hot porridge for the woman and the children. She gave the woman a bag of rice and about two dollars in francs, and the woman was very appreciative. She left and went back to her own village with the kids.

Maybe two months later, the woman returned. She brought Jolie a chicken to say thank you for the help she had given. Mounden was still very skinny, and Jolie could tell he wasn't eating well. Jolie talked to Samedi, and then they offered to let Mounden stay with them in Béré. The woman didn't have enough food to feed the children, and she agreed to let him stay. So, for the past ten years, Mounden has been living with Jolie and Samedi. He calls Jolie "Mama" and Samedi "Papa."

When someone dies here in Chad, it's fairly common for a family member to take in the children of the dead person. But Mounden was the child of a stranger. There was no promise that he would be a good child or that he had anything to offer Samedi and Jolie. Over and over, I'm impressed by their big hearts. We have a lot of kids in our family.

And they wouldn't trade Mounden for anything. He is still extremely skinny. I mean if I didn't know better I would think that no one gave him food. But it's his own fault. Not only does he choose not to bathe, but he is always late to meals. The family eats together, and if you are late, the food will be gone.

This is a hungry bunch. There are never leftovers. He's got to learn.

Mounden is talented with his hands—always rigging something up, fixing flashlights and radios, playing with batteries, arranging wires—anything electric. I gave him some scratched-up CDs that I found and asked him if he could make a hanging mobile that would reflect light for baby Galas to look at. He did it—made it happen.

He took the leftover CDs and drilled holes into the circumferences, inserting little lightbulbs that he'd salvaged from some other ap-

Mounden makes me want to put my hand over my heart. It's what I feel like doing when I feel real love for someone.

pliance. He connected the lights with wires and then hooked them up to a battery. The lights reflect all around the surface of the CDs. I feel proud of him, and he's not even my kid!

When I asked him what he wanted to do for a career, he said, "Be a pilot." I talked to Gary, the mission pilot here, and asked if he could take

Mounden up with him soon. He said he would do it. I can just imagine what it will be like for him! Can you imagine going in a small airplane for the first time?

* * * * *

Mounden and I built a pigeon house the other day.
Yeah.
From the ground up.
Out of mud and sticks.

It's ghetto, *but kingly,* with its flagpole fashioned from fabric scraps that we found on the market streets. To start the building, we hauled water from our well and poured it into holes that we dug down a few feet. We made mud and mucked it up with our feet—a swimming-in-Jello feeling. (I've never actually done that!) We were so dirty and weren't worrying about it. We even put mud on our faces to exaggerate the intensity of our work, telling Samedi that we'd been working *haaaaarrrrrdddddd*!

After stacking mud bricks in disjointed layers, we stood back aways and threw handfuls of mud into the see-through cracks. Next, we rubbed the walls smooth, and I felt proud. Then we laid long sticks side by side, spanning the distance between the walls to make a roof, which we then topped with lots of rice stalks and sealed with more mud. We scratched the name, The Pigeon House, into the mud roof, and it will dry that way.

Mounden rigged some doors and circular pigeon entrances. He bought some pigeons, and I bought some too. We locked them in the house until they learned that it was their home. Now, they happily come back every day and have their little nesting areas in the pigeon quarters.

Brothers are the same around the world—they like to wrestle, have water fights, and trick their sisters into eating dirt. (Mounden!) It's just the most beautiful thing—how time goes by in hours and days without your noticing its passing, and then one day, you blink and realize that someone means a whole lot to you.

The Goodness of Man

Stabs through bone take immeasurable aggression,
and here in my heart I lay out this confession:
that I doubt
and I fear,
Lord, it's not clear what was ever GOOD in man.
But deep in us You called something good.
Some spirit, some desire,
I wish that we could,
reclaim the goodness You placed in us.

I've never been that scared. Each Saturday afternoon our volunteer group has been singing songs in each of the hospital wards. We had just finished singing, and as we came out of the hospital and into the main courtyard area, we noticed some commotion going on in the emergency room. The sky had that bleak, post-sunset lighting, and we were maneuvering carefully around bodies that were lying under the mango trees. We stopped amid some of them and Sarah, a nurse from Denmark, asked somewhat urgently, "Would you guys mind giving us a hand? We need to get these people into the emergency room."

We looked down more carefully and noticed that the people who we thought were merely napping on the ground were actually men, women, and children who had been beaten and were bleeding. The shock we felt as we grappled with the brutality with which these people had been injured made us hesitate. But after some prompting, everyone grabbed hold of the injured people. A few of them could hobble, others couldn't walk at all, and still others were unconscious. Some were already dead.

I scooped up a chubby baby girl whose little dress was completely soaked in blood. Her eyes were wide as the Atlantic, and her body's shock response kept her from crying. I laid her down on the pink emergency-room bed and began looking for injuries, watching her quick breaths, begging them to continue. I cut off that print dress and snipped the ties that held her crocheted beanie on her head. There were no injuries despite all the blood. After a while, her eyes were tracking me. Apparently, the shock had worn off.

The blood that covered her, I came to find out, was from her mother, who had been killed. Who will explain this night to her when she's older and asks why she has no mother? It was a night that would change everything for her.

Eighteen patients were hospitalized that night, and nine or so were taken to our morgue. The violence was sparked when an Arab decided to take his cows across the rice field of a Nangjere. The rice fields and wells are the sources of life here, so I understand that this spoke volumes about how much this Arab cared about the Nangjere. "I'm walking over your hard work. I don't care if you get a good crop." But it's true that the Arab has to get his cows to water one way or another. The cows are the Arabs' source of food. The cows pull their wagons, and the Arabs drink their milk and sell their meat.

Anyway, the Nangjere man yelled at the Arab to get off his field. The Arab became angry and pulled out his bow and arrow. Trying to protect himself, the Nangjere man somehow jumped on the back of the Arab, who pulled his knife from his belt and stabbed him. He fell, and the Nangjere women went running home to tell their families that the Arab had killed their brother!

So, the violence escalated from a couple men swinging at each other to tribal fighting that surged back and forth. The attacks went on all night. First, a wave of Nangjere would come in, and then a wave of Arabs. Then people would seek revenge again, and the cycle would continue. I'd never seen such senselessness with my own eyes.

Women beaten so badly that every inch of their faces was swollen.
Knife wounds in their heads.
Pregnant women!

Part Three: The Goodness of Man

One man was attacked while he was fishing.
He was just catching fish, that's all.
And his Nangjere ethnicity made him a target.

His wounds told the whole story. A knife had left trails across his shoulders, down his back, and across his butt. Someone had been ruthlessly slashing him as he ran. Then you could see that he must have gotten tired. He probably couldn't run anymore, or maybe he felt that running couldn't save him. He must have turned around to confront his attacker because there were deep cuts all across his wrists, hands, and arms, and into his lung. (He ended up with a chest tube.) Someone monitored his vitals and held compresses deep in his wounds until the doctor was free to stitch them up. The night was spent anticipating the next wave of revenge.

By 2 A.M. the police felt they had enough of a presence that the fighting would stop. The patients had been settled on plastic mattresses, and the dead were at the morgue. The orphaned and unidentified babies had been given to families who would nurse them for the night. Things had settled a bit. Everything except my insides—my gut.

I didn't sleep that night.
I was too disappointed in humanity.
Too scared of humans.
Too tired of being a human on this earth.

I went to Ansley's hut so I wouldn't have to sleep alone, and I cried. What kind of person strikes someone else with a knife so hard that it cuts through that person's bone and breaks it? I thought that deep down inside, people were good. But this—this was challenging a huge pillar of my thinking. I love people. I always feel like there is something good in every person and that you just have to find it. But that night I honestly was just so disappointed.

The next day at the hospital was tense. A mob of Arabs came in to pick up their dead. As they entered the hospital grounds, we saw Nangjere jumping the fence out of the hospital. All of us stood paralyzed as we saw them move across the courtyard; there was an understandable fear that they were going to take revenge by killing those who were healing at the hospital. Then guards came and took positions at the hospital—holding rifles on their shoulders.

41

The patients healing side by side—Arab and Nangjere, bed by bed. It all spoke of the senselessness. The injuries and deaths painted a really ugly picture of revenge. I hope it affected everyone as it did me. Humanity? Now I'm not sure who we are. I'm searching, uncertain and uneasy.

i am a disco dancer

I stood in the marketplace with Daniel, a friend and Chadian teacher of French at the high school across town. While we waited for Ansley to meet us, a crowd began to gather. They circled round us and, crossing their arms, whispered to their friends in dialect about my skin and clothes and hair and eyes. No one asked, "Where are you from?" or "What's your name?" Nope. Just good old, silent, arms-crossed staring. I don't mean only three people either. One person staring seems to give permission for twenty-five others to join in.

I'm used to it by now, but sometimes I just want to give them something to look at. I've contemplated dancing wildly, singing a loud solo really off tune, or just running at them, screaming like a crazy girl. I'm uninteresting really. I felt like their time was being wasted as they commented on my uneventful existence, but I just stood there anyway.

Then Daniel said something that struck a beautiful chord in me. Even though he is a local, because he was waiting there with me, he also found himself at the center of this ring. He looked quizzically at those who were staring and kindly asked in French, "What are you looking at, kids? She is a person just like you." With giggles and smirks, the crowd realized the truth in what Daniel said and began to turn away in embarrassment.

Right before I came to Chad, my twenty-year-old brother Fletcher, his sweet, red-headed girlfriend Laura, my dad, and I went to the autumn fair where I live. Fletcher and Laura's aura of love and the way my dad hyped up the tractors, horse barns, and lumberjack show made for an evening full of fun dynamics and memorable conversation.

Fletcher, Laura, and I craved a funnel cake. But when we got to the booth, the line was long—especially in comparison to the line for elephant ears. We decided funnel cake was worth the wait anyway.

Eventually, the wall of greasy hot air hit us, and we knew we were getting close to the front of the line. We'd been standing there with other would-be feasters for at least twenty minutes, so I was starting to feel a bond with them. I decided I would comment on our common situation. I leaned toward the girl ahead of me and said, "Wow, I almost caved in and just got an elephant ear, but I'm sure glad I didn't!" The girl totally didn't hear me. Or maybe she just completely ignored me. Either way, I was left hanging on my last word, waiting for a response that wasn't coming. Fletcher and Laura laughed hysterically at my very unsuccessful attempt to connect to that girl. Failed connection!

However, standing on common ground is awesome. Sometimes, here in Africa, it's like, "Wow, we're from really different worlds. What do we have in common?" But then we'll connect over some odd and funny thing, such as when little Armelle, three years old, felt my prickly, unshaven legs and then compared them to her own, or when Mounden sang, "I am a disco dancer," at the top of his lungs, or when we played soccer out in the blazing sun behind the church in our bare feet.

Connection! Gotta keep trying to connect to people—even if you get shut down from time to time. Even if your attempts fail. The few times when sparks fly and you, for a few seconds, actually feel like you're reading the same page of the same book and laughing at the same parts as those around you . . . so worth it.

Dinga's heart

Dinga is my African sister. Her fragile body whispers grace as she moves around tending our home. She weighs a mere eighty pounds.

Though small, Dinga has a big presence. Though uneducated, she is extremely smart. And though she doesn't speak French, of all the family members, she's the one I hear loudest and clearest.

Dinga's family lives across town. I don't fully understand why she lives with us, but we were both adopted by this family, and maybe that's why I like sleeping next to her on the big mat. She never asks for more blanket during the night, always takes less than half of the pillow, and rarely kicks me or hits me in her sleep.

She isn't in school; she's husband-shopping weekly—lining them up on benches outside the mud wall and bringing them tea, sesame balls, and peanut-butter soup. What qualities she's looking for I'm not sure; she and the boys rarely exchanged more than jokes, and I've gathered these are only the preliminaries—the tryouts if you will. Perhaps there have been follow-up visits that I haven't seen.

Dinga sings this out-of-tune yet oddly melodic string of notes, and she holds babies constantly. In the evenings, she tells me my hair is a mess and then braids it in ways that never look good on me. My temples always burn after all her yanking of hair in those sensitive places. I try not to whine; but there I am—always crying but not sad.

Dinga used to wash the dishes—until she realized that I knew how to do that. Now she says, *"Emily pulka tassé"* (Emily, wash the dishes!) So now that's my job—scrubbing crusty rice out of blackened pots.

"I want to be fat," Dinga tells me. Then, pointing to her frail body, she says, "This not good." She's a gem. Yes, she's as valuable as the most precious gem you could think of.

But Dinga has a bigger problem than her weight. Though she's just fourteen, her heart beats out of her chest. Some days, it beats in good rhythm—consistent, reliable, and strong. Other days Dinga looks literally brokenhearted. At those times you can ask her questions and she won't hear you, or at best, she'll nod without caring what the question was.

Her heart, defective from birth, beats arrhythmically, skipping beats and pounding against her ribs, visibly moving them. Every time it happens when I'm there—I hate it that it is so often—I'm helpless, *wishing* I could steady it. Her lips shake and quiver, she shivers, and her eyes flash despair. Often she grabs my hand and places it on my chest, where I can feel what's happening.

Bam.

Bam-bam.

Bam-bam-bam-bam.

I know feeling someone's heart beat through their skin is nothing compared to having that heart in your own body and having to feel every beat it makes.

Once I woke up in the middle of the night, and Dinga was gasping—her shoulders rising and falling in painful rhythm with her breathing, attempting to keep pace with her heart—which can be completely unpredictable. I panicked and asked, *"Ca va?"* She replied, *"Ca va di,"* combining French with the negative of this region's dialect. She was saying, "It goes not."

It goes not for her.

Seriously not going.

Not well, anyway.

I asked if she wanted water, wanted to lie down, wanted my blanket. Solution, where are you?

The heart is so deep in the body. If it were a matter of a cut on her foot, no problem. If it were a superficial burn, we'd do something about it. But how do we get to her heart? It's a bigger problem than Africa is equipped to deal with.

rusty pink

The hospital has a payment plan that allows people to leave some object of value—their bike, metal pot, or cell phone—as collateral until they return to pay their bill. They have two months to pay off their debt. Some people decide simply to leave whatever they've left as collateral rather than pay to reclaim it. When the two months have passed, the hospital assumes the property and sells it to pay the medical bill for which it stood as collateral.

The hospital had a "yard sale" yesterday, and I joined everyone who was buying the collateral that people had abandoned. I bought this rusty, pink antique bike. When I brought it home, my African family laughed at it—they told me it was such a bad bike! Sabine, who is eighteen and has signed up to be my critic while I'm here, laughed and said, "I'm really sorry for you, Emily. *Desólé*, Emily."

But, Jago, eighteen and optimistic, told me he would help me get it fixed up. We went to the market later in the day. Jago told me to pretend the bike was his so I wouldn't get ripped off, so I played some tagalong white girl while he bought the parts. We had a good act going. We got the bike all fixed up for the fair price of about twenty dollars, and I rode it home.

New tires.

New pedals.

New seat.

My bike has two great features. First, the bell. It rings in a dull, halting bullet sort of a sound—but it rings nonetheless. Second, it has a rather fragile-looking rack that hovers over the back tire. A second person can sit on that rack and ride along with their legs straddled on either side of the back wheel. I plan on taking it to the river all the time. Every day. And I can take a friend along. It's perfect.

There is one downside to the bike. It has no brakes. It's not even like they're just broken—they don't exist. Of course, Chad is undeniably flat, so maybe I'm safe. And perhaps the lack of brakes is the reason for the bell. Instead of stopping, I simply ring the bell and everyone gets out of my way. These small, joyful things, like bikes and bells, really shine up this place that is sometimes so dark.

pass it on

Soooooo, Stephan found me yesterday and said a slight bit frantically, "Emily, I made a mistake and sold you that bike. The person who owns it is here to pay it off and pick it up. You have to give it back. I'm really sorry." Stephan had thought the hospital had already had the bike for two months, so I bought it for eight thousand francs, which is about sixteen dollars. Not a bad deal.

I took the bike and got everything on it fixed—for an additional ten thousand francs (twenty dollars). After it was fixed up, even my family, who had said it was a bad bike, *loved* my pink bike. So when Stephan told me I had to give it back, I just had to laugh. It had been a nice bike rental.

This man is carrying his wife and child home from the hospital on his bike.

I took the bike to the family who owned it as they waited outside the hospital office. I watched their faces brighten up as they realized their old junk bike had received a complete makeover. They didn't know what to say. They had beaming smiles of gratitude. We took a picture together with the bike, and as they were leaving, they thanked me effusively.

I wish I knew how to say "Pass it on" in French—pass on the favor. Meanwhile, I'm missing my bike, and the walk to the river is really long.

blood in my mouth

Rubber suction bulbs were stitched into both lower quadrants of his abdomen. They filled almost every hour with post-surgery bleeding and drainage, and it was critical that they be emptied regularly lest the fluids accumulate and distend his belly.

Ideally, I'd be heroic—approach the wincing patient confidently, empty the suction bulb, calmly reengage the suction, make note of the milliliters discharged, and knowledgeably assure the family that the patient is on the track to recovery. But more often, that is *far* from the case. I find myself less than courageous, stepping back from bloody messes, and wanting companionship when addressing intense suffering. I'm scared of being alone at death and at moments of great sadness.

Today, when I unplugged the suction bulb of the man's lower left quadrant, intending to empty it, blood sprayed into my mouth. I instinctively spat it onto the cement, while my mind flooded with thoughts of HIV and other blood-borne pathogens. Here, as I'm still at the beginning of my experience, I have so much fear—both legitimate and illegitimate fear.

sisters-in-law

Last night I worked the night shift. About 11 P.M. a man came in with his foot bleeding a bit like a river flows. He hadn't brought any record of medical history, no money, and as he told me what happened, his breath was hot with alcohol. To make his long story short, he had gotten into a fight with his sister-in-law. She had taken a rice blade to his foot in anger, and his brother brought him to the hospital four hours later. I couldn't help but laugh just a little bit—what a sister-in-law he's got. Then I remembered that I'm going to have a sister-in-law very soon! Taylor, my older brother, is getting married a few weeks after I get back to the States, and I'll get a sister! Yippee! Then I think again and start trembling at the thought. I've just seen evidence of how crazy a sister-in-law can be. Yikes!

Girls have always liked Taylor. He has a kind, reassuring presence, but he also projects a feeling of quiet mystery. He's also stolen my friends, who then morphed into his girlfriends! But Nilmini—he found her on his own. And the lottery has been won, people—Nil is so awesome.

So after this guy tromps all over our emergency room, dripping blood everywhere and almost falling over, I got him to sit down *outside*. Samedi and I soaked his foot in a blue basin full of bleach water and then scrubbed it well. Samedi put stitches in, and I bandaged it up. He went home that night, and we laughed when he was gone.

Sisters-in-law—yikes!

their thing

I was talking to my parents on the phone this morning and told them that I had overcome my fear of riding horses alone here in Chad—and more specifically, of riding them to the river by myself. My dad said, "Emily, you really shouldn't go to the water alone. Take someone with you when you go."

I pretend to resent being looked after—I spout off things about my age and how big a number it is, how independent and safe I am, and how I am never in any danger. But in my secret thoughts, at least some parts of me greatly appreciate my father's care.

This morning I saddled Libby and was riding the west road out of the village when Samedi saw me.

"Emily, where are you going?"

"I'm going to the river."

"Who are you going with?"

"Myself."

"Emily, that's not safe. It's better if you go with someone else."

"That's what my real father said too. But don't worry! I know how to swim."

With a shake of his head and the use of my favorite French phrase—"*Toi là,*" meaning "You there"—he wished me well.

Libby trotted choppily past lots of dogs. They spooked her badly, putting her on edge for the rest of the ride. When I ride past dogs, I just make sure we are running really fast—the sooner we get by them, the better, because if they nip Libby's heel, I'm done for.

Part Three: The Goodness of Man

When we reached the river, Libby was sweaty and tired. I tied her to a bush using a very creative knot: I weave the rope around branches and leaves and then I just believe in it—believe it will hold.

I was alone at the river, so it was quiet and I could talk to Libby and not feel stupid. Walking to the edge of the river, I stripped to my swimming suit and waded up to my waist—that chilly point—and then dived in. So cold, and so appreciated! I dunked my head, keeping my lips tightly sealed (the cleanliness of the water is iffy), paddled against the current for a while, and then swam across the river to a dusty, beachish place—almost sandy—where I stretched out.

My mind went from thinking about the water quality of the river to my faucet at home, to the flies that were landing on my eyelashes, to hippos—and at that point I started hearing things. Glancing up, I saw people approaching.

Have you ever met people who were just doing their thing and whatever their thing was, it was just inspiring because of how they were doing it? It's not like their thing was some big, amazing thing. It's just something about *the way* they do their thing.

These ladies approaching me were doing their thing. Each of them was carrying a load of long, skinny branches—firewood. I couldn't have gotten my arms around one of those bundles if I tried. They weren't bundles of kindling. No sirree. Each stick was like seven feet tall. Each woman looked like a stick herself—four sticks dressed in big baggy shorts, carrying sticks. As they got to the river, I realized that they were going to cross. They hiked their baggy shorts up around their stickish legs and strode slowly through the water, leaning into the current, all the while balancing the bundles on their heads.

I called out to them, *"Mn loogia buja!"* (You work a lot!)

They called back, *"Oo Oo!"* (Yes! Yes!)

"Mn pulkaga?" they asked me. (You are bathing?)

"On pulkaba. Joge joge on ma dikuna," I replied. (I bathed already. Now, I'm going to sleep.)

"Mn gba pulka danga?" I asked. (Will you come and bathe too?)

At that they leaned their big bundles teepee-style around a tree at the river's edge and came to join me.

So here we are, in this dirty river, bathing together. They stalled with the water at waist level. I told them they should get all the way in, that it felt good. But they replied, *"Kala Buja!"* (Freezing cold!)

After a while of this funny small talk, I said I was going back over to my beach to sleep. When I got there, I did a snow angel in the sand. They thought that was funny. Obviously, being in Africa, they've never seen children play in snow.

"Weinda, soor shaiga?"

An invitation to tea tomorrow. They told me where to meet them and told me to come anytime in the afternoon. That, I would love.

Then they raised their firewood to their heads again and chatted as they started out briskly on their hour-long walk to the market. Just doing their thing—I love that way they were doing their thing.

calling death

Today, when a woman died, Samedi told me to take her pulse. I felt her right wrist and said, "There isn't one," but then the responsibility of pronouncing death being too much for me to bear alone, I asked Samedi to take her pulse too.

Pronouncing death feels almost like killing. Who wants to be the one to say there's no hope for life here—to give up, to decide it's over? No one signs up for that, yet when someone does die, pretending that he or she didn't won't fool anyone for long. Sometimes I think that maybe I'm just not finding the right place on the person's wrist, the place where the pulse might be felt. But no, this person is really dead. We announce births and welcome the newborn, and at the end, we say goodbye and say the benediction. I'm learning about death's arrival, and it's hard—so hard.

a good whipping

A confident child followed me, after I called his name, into the emergency room. He climbed up, dropped his pants so they hung around his ankles, and sat bare-butted on the salmon-colored examination table. He had obviously done this numerous times. And there on his thigh was a bandage that he had come to have changed. I peeled the grippy tape back carefully and then remembered how much more it hurts to pull Band-Aids off slowly. The tape they use here sticks so well to dry skin. In fact, as I peeled it off, the top layer of brown epidermis came off too.

When the dressing was off, I saw a clean slice about three inches long on his upper thigh. It was almost healed and mostly scarred over. The dressing change required only washing the healed wound with bleach water and scrubbing some of the dirt from around the edges. It really looked quite good.

I asked him if it hurt as I washed it. He said, "No, it's OK," and I believed him because he didn't flinch or wince. As I put another piece of tape over the wound, I asked him how it had happened—I thought it was a weird place for an injury like this. He said, "My teacher hit me."

Bleh—sick feeling.

This kid had to come to the hospital because his teacher hit him with a stick. The stick had cleanly laid open his leg. I didn't know this kid or his potential for bad behavior or what he had done that might have provoked his teacher to hit him like that—but it didn't matter. I had only ill thoughts of that teacher, and my blood pressure went up. I finished my shift and went home.

I usually sigh out my anxiety when I enter our cluster of huts, because all the pain of the hospital is countered by a wash of good things at this home of mine: visitors drinking tea, babies gnawing on green mangoes, Jolie and her jovial songs, children tugging on my fingers, that strong feeling of belonging, the sweet air of community. But today was different. The air was silently angry, and no one was moving much—just tensely standing around.

I pretended not to notice and gathered my things to shower. As I walked toward the little mud enclosure, I heard some commotion. I turned around and saw Izeedoor, thirteen, and Tony, eleven, arguing with each other. Then, out of nowhere, Jezue, the oldest of Samedi's children who are still living at home, came onto the scene with speed and fury. I have never seen him like that. Usually he is so kind, so compassionate and loving. I froze behind the bathroom wall, peering over it.

Jezue started whipping both of the boys and yelling things I didn't understand. His first stroke broke the stick he was swinging on Izeedoor's shoulder. I whimpered instinctively and clutched my shower basket—eyes locked on my brothers. The next few hits made all my muscles tense up. Tony escaped, running out through the field, but Izeedoor got caught by the neck of his shirt and dragged under the central tree in our courtyard. With his free hand, Jezue broke off a branch from the neem tree, and Izeedoor got the whipping of his life.

I couldn't watch. I felt like I couldn't stop this. People whom I

51

respected a lot were simply letting this situation play out—people like Jolie and Esther and Salmon. I backed into my hut and sat on the edge of my cot in my shower robe, just listening to the symphony of cries and hits and pleas. Since then I've sat like that on the edge of my cot quite a few times after shocking situations here in Béré. It's becoming familiar.

When the screaming stopped, it was replaced by crying. Full-out sobbing. I came quietly out of my hut and walked over to where Jolie sat. I asked her why Izeedoor was treated like this. She told me that Izeedoor had insulted his uncle, Jezue, and that he is little and needs to respect his elders. She said that it was good that he got this beating.

I told her it was not good for my heart—*"Ce n'est pas bon pour mon coeur."* She nodded sympathetically, letting me know that she understood. Izeedoor hid behind the tree literally for the next two hours, and no one talked. I wanted to go over and hug him. But to be respectful of the culture, I needed to let him cry.

Or did I? Just because something is *cultural* doesn't mean it's *right*. I'm learning that this is true. I am also learning that *because* something is cultural, you *have to* understand the culture before you pass judgment on it or try to change it, and I'm still gaining understanding.

But deep down—no, actually, not that deep down—pretty superficially, fairly clearly, I felt that being whipped *so* hard and with such uncontrolled anger was wrong.

As I talked with Samedi this morning over breakfast, I said, "Samedi, I have so many questions but I don't have enough French to understand the answers yet." He laughed and said, "You'll get there, Emily." I know I will, but I'm so impatient.

Part Four

Bed Four of Twelve

There is a young mother in bed four of twelve. She's suffering a bad bout of malaria and a cough that racks her body. It's what they call a productive cough; it's producing mucus and phlegm, which she spits into a rag and tucks it in between the bed frame and mattress.

She doesn't cover her mouth when she coughs, and when the sun slips in through the window at just the right angle, you can see her coughs sending a dense spray whichever way she's facing. She is being looked after by an inconsistent smattering of family members who come in but don't bring her anything. Her nine-year-old daughter sleeps below the metal bed at night, all balled up with her hands between her thighs.

Some tired nurse ran a blood clot out of the young woman's IV tubing and right onto the ground beside the bed leg. It's dried now, and it's got neighboring filth all around, including crumbs of sugar crackers, rat droppings, and rings where a puddle of something used to sit.

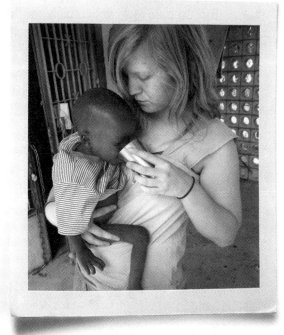

Sometimes I think these babies will melt the plastic mattresses they lie on. Their burning, malaria-infested bodies radiate heat.

53

She coughs, and the spray settles on her six-month-old baby. He resembles her, not in looks really, but in health. However, his cough screams high above the tone of hers. Oh, and his ribs clench down over the lungs in an oppressive sort of way. While his bones are probably like anyone else's, they look much sharper because they're so close to his skin's surface. The bare form looks like a child in a hand-me-down jumpsuit—his skin is way too big for him.

The nurse walks over to the IV pole to change the perfusion and clips the baby's foot with her body as she brushes by the bed. Then she glances over her shoulder, becoming aware of the baby, who is now crying.

Perhaps it's because of the way the mother's arms lie limply under the baby and her eyes never look at him, but you'd hardly know something valuable belonged to her, much less another heartbeat. She is exhausted and has little strength to give.

cartwheels

I swung Aaron around by his arms today. It seemed like no one had ever done that to him before. That "trick" seemed to begin what became stunt time. Everyone in my family had some trick to perform! Some did handstands, some made funny faces, and some moved their bodies through incredible dance routines.

And Jolie did a cartwheel! This sweet, homemaking African mother clothed in her traditional African wrap did an impressive bent-legged cartwheel! I cheered in both shock and love. Jolie and I have so many commonalities, and as they are uncovered, I've begun to wonder how many other people who I thought were very different are actually similar. Jolie and I grew up in two very different ways, but we both love cartwheels.

let me take your temperature

Sometimes I think these babies will melt the plastic mattresses that they lie on. Their burning, malaria-infested bodies radiate heat to their mothers or whoever holds them. And taking their temperatures is sometimes a challenge. Thermometers somehow continually disappear. They often break too. I've broken a couple glass thermometers myself, and last night there were none left. Steffan, the administrative assistant, said there were none in the storage room either. I wasn't sure what exactly would be the best plan of action for my night shift, but I decided to take temperatures as best I could.

The next morning, as I gave my report to the day nurse, she asked me what the Yeses and Nos were doing in the column that should hold temperatures. I explained that I had to go by touch because there were no thermometers in the house. I felt the babies' chests and heads, and if they felt like they were burning up, I put a Yes in the column and ordered the family to bring wet cloths for the baby. If the baby's body felt like mine, then I'd write No.

So often we're short staffed and short supplied, but we're trying. We're definitely trying.

bitter defensive

Over and over and over.

It happened again.

I want to lay it out for you clearly: this situation that seems to play out over and over and over again.

A mother and father come to the hospital with an extremely sick child. They pay for the consultation. The doctor tells them what the child needs to get better: Blood transfusion. Medicated perfusions. Hospitalization.

The parents say, "We don't have the money."

That's almost everyone's response, because really, honestly, what money they have could *easily* go to another basic need of theirs. Oil and rice. A T-shirt to alternate with the one they have. School bills.

Most parents have some money, but not much of it. I know that sometimes parents have said they don't have any money but then, when they see that no one is going to pay for them, they pull money out of their pockets and put it on the table. It is SO hard to tell who really needs the money.

I'm learning that paying for every child's hospital bill would take away the honorable and appropriate responsibility of parents to take care of their children. It's true. If parents learn that they don't have to take responsibility for their children, that someone else will pick up the slack for them,

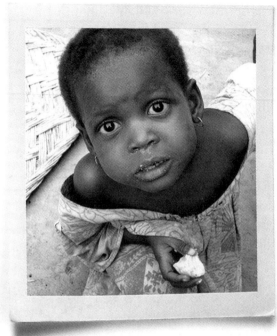

Should we give parents a break when they really can't pay for their child's treatment? Do we step in only when the child is about to die?

they could begin to depend on that.

But when do we give parents a break when they really don't have the money? When do we say, "You *do* need help"? Do we step in only when they're about to die of starvation? Do we wait for them to walk out of the doors of the hospital because they can't pay and then run after them and say, "OK, OK, OK, so you really don't have money. Come back in here"? It is just hard to know where to draw the line when *everyone* is struggling.

I was presenting the patients to Dr. Francois,* an intern from Togo, during rounds the other day, and the baby in the first bed was sick with malaria and extremely malnourished. Fever, respiratory infection, vomiting, and dehydration. The doctor took a look at the chart and wrote down what needed to be done and I explained it to the father. He said, "This is too much. I don't have the money for this. We must go home."

Dr. Francois in French instantly laid into him. "You want to leave the hospital when your baby is like this? Do you understand that he will die?"

The man said, "We don't have the money."

Dr. Francois said, "Do you want your child to get better? Do you? Do you?"

Avoiding eye contact, the man said quietly, "If I had the money, this would be simple. But it's not simple."

My heart went out to the man because I really think he was telling the truth. But the doctor was frustrated, I could tell. He sees so many people scamming to get free care at the hospital—people who could pay but just don't want to.

*Not his real name.

The doctor said, "OK, give me your medical *carne*. I'll discharge you if that's what you want!"

The man slowly handed over the little yellow medical records book.

The doctor said, "This is on you! This is not my fault. This is not the hospital's fault. YOU are deciding to leave—it's your fault!" And with that, he wrote the discharge orders for the little boy.

The man seemed so sad. He hung his head and, frustratedly, said, "Yes. I know. I understand. It's on me. It's all because of me."

I asked the doctor if I could talk to him. We left the ward, and I asked him if he really thought the man actually had money. He said, "Yes. Maybe."

I said I really didn't think he did. The man was handicapped. His feet were just knobs, having been amputated or malformed at birth, and he walked with a crutch. His clothes were old, with holes scattered about, and while these things are not sure signs of poverty, they certainly were indicators.

I asked the doctor again, "So, you really think he has money?" He said Yes, and I said OK. He went back in and finalized the process of sending the man home with his dying child. And home they went.

It still gets me.

Was that the right thing to do? Or are we so bitter and defensive that we can't recognize need? It is one of the hardest things about this place.

when you hit rock

Izeedoor chomped on a rock in the rice tonight. In pain, he cupped his mouth with his hand, spit out what he'd been chewing, and shook his head, and the clash of rock on teeth was a nice little prelude to the stream of complaints that came from his mouth then. EVERYONE turned and pointed at Esther, who had done a poor job of preparing the rice. With grins and chuckles, they commented about her ability to cook. Everyone thought it was funny—everyone except Izeedoor. And Esther. She acted sheepish.

Esther is generally confident, but I can tell she's working to meet her culture's expectations of her as a woman. Girls grow to be women . . . don't we?

I told my brother Fletcher never to use the word *woman* to call to a girl.

He said, "But you *are* a woman." I explained that somehow we girls have been robbed of that word in its original meaning. *Woman* has a bad feel to it because too many men have used it to demand things—that their wives bring them food or whatever.

What do I want to be called? I don't know. *Lady* sounds frumpy, and *girl* sounds youngish. I want the word *woman* back I guess.

And while the women here in Chad are fairly dependent on the men at times (money), men are also very dependent on women. And being a woman is an incredibly noble thing—women knit society together, raising children and running the marketplace, caring for the sick and providing meals.

Esther is becoming a woman. I can tell she wants to serve the family food that has no rocks in it.

sipping and passing

Last night I woke up in the dark with a screaming thirst. It was the same kind I remember from when I was a kid—when I'd wake up in the middle of the night and be so thirsty that even while still half asleep, I would walk to the bathroom sink, turn on the faucet, and with my eyes still closed, lap up water out of my cupped hands like a puppy. You just do it because your body tells you to. And last night, there was no option of going back to sleep.

So, I climbed out my mosquito net, quietly sneaked out of my hut, and shuffled my bare feet over to the well. I found the long rope and followed it to the end where the bucket was, dropped the bucket in the well, and hauled up some water. I can draw water up just fine now—even in the dark.

Holding the bucket with both hands, I tipped it back and drank. There was sand on the bucket's lip and now on my lips, and the water tasted like dirt. But just like those days when I was a kid, I walked back to bed satisfied.

When I first moved in with this family, I always bottled up clean water at the hospital and brought it home. The water there is pumped from deep in the ground and doesn't have the gut-turning bacteria called *Giardia*. The kids knew I didn't drink water from our open well, and I was kind of sheepish because of that—I felt like a sissy, really. But I explained it to them in terms of my stomach being wimpy; I said that they had strong stomachs, but mine would revolt. At mealtimes, I'd have this "special" water, and the kids loved to drink it.

Slowly, though, as time has passed here, I've accepted some new normals.

Being barefoot is preferable—especially for jogging.

The smell of other people's urine while showering is OK.

While I'm definitely still careful, blood is less scary.

Having a baby wet your lap while you hold it is funny, and your clothes dry just fine.

Sifting bugs out of flour and picking them out of bread is no longer worth the effort.

Grasshoppers make a fine dessert.

Clothes can be worn two days in a row.

And I drink our well water now.

"You drink it now, Emily? Your stomach is strong now?" the kids ask.

We pass wooden bowls of water around at mealtimes, and everyone sips and passes, sips and passes.

dressing changes

When I change dressings on people's wounds, my eyes tense up, my eyebrows angle downward, and my forehead wrinkles in horizontal stripes. We mix a cap of bleach with a jar full of water, and with that we clean people's wounds. How that bleach must sting as it sterilizes the tender tissues! I imagine it to be awful. But I know the pain leads to a healed foot, an abdomen that can carry another baby, or a collapsed lung that can actually hold air again. There is a song by Relient K that says, "The end will justify the pain it took to get us there." Still, when I stuff stinging gauze into a two-inch-deep hole in the side of someone's leg, I can't always stop my face from taking that shape.

moon walk

Aaron's head is cozied up on my lap, and Armelle can't stop running her hand along my prickly, unshaven leg. Night has fallen, and our energy levels have as well. In fact, Armelle's stroking begins to slow down, and her eyes lose that look of wonder as she slips out of consciousness.

My French is better now. Our conversations can be interesting and can even reflect opinion, emotion, and breadth of topic. With so many of us lying in the hut, it's not often that conversation dies.

Tonight, the moon is especially massive.
And we don't need flashlights.
That big ball of light does a better job.
The moon demands some acknowledgment tonight.

"You know someone has walked on that," I say, referring to the bright, rocky surface of the moon. Tony sits up from where he is stretched out and says, "Really? Up there?" And Esther's face speaks for her mouth and tells me that she's never heard this fact before. They ask about humanity's ascent to and stroll on the moon's surface—they have a hard time believing me.

Education. I've taken it for granted.
The sight of children,
the other night,
lying on their stomachs
in the dirt
around a lamp
with their prized notebooks,
teaching each other math.
Twelve-year-olds,
teaching seven-year-olds.

It's not ideal, really—the education system. The schools vary—the public grade school is simply a thatch roof with see-through thatch walls. Inside, the children learn orally while they sit on mud bricks that lift them maybe three inches off the dirt.

Education, when you are in a third-world village, is something you have to want in order to get it.

You have to clutch at it.

Seek it.

Reach for it.

And even then, you might not get it.

By the time that middle-class American children are ten, they know what dinosaurs are and how incredibly large the ocean is. By the age of thirteen, they know people need protein and how blood circulates in the body. By the age of sixteen, they know about chemical reactions and the speed of light. All along they learn world history and local history, and news is available everywhere.

And here I am breaking the news that men have walked on the moon! It's a privilege and a really special moment.

sleepover

Estella is the baby of the family. Her eyes lock onto those of others unapologetically. She doesn't shift them sideways or worry that she might be thought to be staring because at seven years old, you're allowed deviations from most social rules. Energy is stacked behind her eyes, waiting for any chance to ignite. And when her eyes find yours, they crease and bend and squint about and her smile does the same. Then her body starts bobbing—springing from her toes—that soon turns into full-on explosions of her legs UP and DOWN! And somehow, even while she is moving up and down, her eyes never leave yours. And it's not awkward at all. I think that is what joy looks like.

Estella's twelve-year-old sister, Merci, makes perfect grades at school, exudes confidence, and is more levelheaded, often trying to tame Estella's behavior. But from time to time, she herself ditches her maturity and screams loudly or spontaneously contorts her face to get a reaction.

Their mom's name is Brigette. She wears her clothes haphazardly, paying little attention to how she dresses—like she isn't trying. Head-wraps always sweep her forehead, and long, flashy earrings dangle and distract me when we talk. She's older, but she has the same energy that Estella does. Her eyes do that same lighty thing, only it's a bit more con-trolled. It seems like her eyes have more experience, have seen more hard things than Estella's have, and that knowledge affects her reactions.

Tonight, I came home about 8 P.M., and everyone was spread out on mats in front of *my hut*—which was unusual. I never understand how we decide where to eat the nightly meal. Most of the time, we eat by the cook-ing corner, but then there are random nights when the family spreads their mats out on top of the drying bricks and eats there, and nights when no one eats, and nights when no one is even home.

So when a night like tonight comes and everyone decides to eat outside my door, it catches me by surprise but I'm not really surprised. There are just hundreds of things that I don't understand. I feel like my family must think I ask a million pointless questions. Why do you drink from bowls when you have cups? Why do you drop coals in the tea when it is done? Where do the boys go during the evenings? Who are the random old people who come to visit and don't say a word? Where does everyone go to use the bathroom when we don't have one in our house?

I've never needed to ask so many questions—there's never been so many things that I didn't know. But tonight I didn't even ask why we were eating in a different place, because three-year-old Armelle came sleepily over to me, looking very crisp in her newly sewn holiday dress, but quietly complaining that she was cold. She handed me one of Jolie's wraps—a large piece of cloth—and wanted to be wrapped in it. I tucked one end under her little armpit, and she spun in a circle while the fabric wound around her in tight layers. In this mummified state, she tipped over, flopping down across my lap, which entertained everyone. She fell asleep quickly, and her limp weight cut off the circulation to my feet. She was so cute that I didn't want to move, so my toes went numb.

A few minutes later, Ferdina came running in and said Brigette and her husband were fighting. We all got up and went to our courtyard wall. Brigette met us there, slightly out of breath. She had run barefoot from her house and stood there with her arms crossed, nervously glancing over her shoulder into the dark. She said that her husband was really angry and had hit her—and Estella and Merci were still at home with him.

Brigette drinks rice wine every day. It makes her laugh and smell like alcohol. She's never out of control or thoughtless, but she's definitely more free with her words, and she talks close to my face, which is why I know what her breath smells like.

Apparently, she had gone to the market and slept there all day, leaving the kids alone at home. That's not particularly unusual in Chad, but her husband didn't like it. I'm sure their fight involved an accumulation of other things as well.

Brigette's husband told her, "I don't want you anymore." When she said this, I imagined someone telling me they didn't want me anymore, and despite anything she had done that might have cause him to feel this way, my heart went out to her.

So, in my totally broken Nangjere, I said, "Brigette, I like you a lot. You can stay with me in my hut tonight. I have two beds." At this, Jolie wrapped me up in a hug and burst into laughter, and so did everyone else. I didn't understand what was funny. I laughed a little with them, but I was thinking, *What? I was serious!*

I assumed that they were laughing because I was trying to speak Nangjere. I mostly make jokes when I speak in that dialect—jokes about the food or boyfriends. I don't often use it to communicate meaningful things because, let's get real, it's challenge enough for me to communicate meaningful things in French, and I know much less of the dialect than I do French.

Brigette came in and "hid" with us in our courtyard for a while until Samedi came home. When he got there, everyone pitched in with details of the story.

Samedi's nickname is "Papa Sam." I trust him lots because he is one of the kindest and wisest people I've met. He gets up and checks our doors three times each night to make sure we're safe—said it's his duty as the father. However, more than just doing his duty, I sense that he feels things in his heart and acts out of that. He's given me encouragement many times and talked with me about the things that have upset me or that I don't understand. And it's not just me. He is constantly making peace in the village and taking time for people who come to ask for advice. After hearing the story, Samedi said, "OK, I'll go and talk with your husband," and he left.

He didn't return for a long time, and we got tired of waiting. I told Brigette I was going to bed and said my offer was serious and she could stay with me for the night. She did. I moved my things off the little cot and she lay down. I tried to give her a blanket, but she said she just needed her strip of fabric. Feeling excited to be hosting a sleepover, I settled onto my cot and got ready to talk.

I love to talk at night before I go to sleep. When I was younger, I used to sleep on my older brother Taylor's floor and talk his ear off. Then, when Taylor grew up, went to high school and college, he was never home, so I'd sleep on my younger brother Fletcher's floor. I talked his ear off too. In fact, sometimes Fletcher would say, "Emily, if you're going to sleep in here, you can't talk. I want to sleep." Ha! It's just that when I lie down at night, my mind starts up and I think of everything important.

So I started talking to Brigette as we lay there in the dark. She answered a few things and then said, "OK, Emily, sleep. It's time to sleep." I laughed inside and almost out loud because even when you come to a completely new place, some parts of you follow, as if they're attached by a string.

A while later, Samedi knocked on my door. He said he had just talked to Brigette's husband, and that after a lot of convincing, he had decided that he wouldn't hit Brigette and that he would take her back. Brigette got up and said she would go home.

When she left, she shut the door behind her, and Samedi said, "Emily, you should lock your door." I told him that the lock didn't work from the inside. He said, "What! It hasn't worked all this time? Well, you should put something in front of the door then," and he brought me a brick to put in front of it. Of course, that isn't going to keep anyone out, but I love the fact that they're looking out for me!

Josephine

Josephine, a new admittee, started panicking soon after we got her into a bed. She was hollering that there was a dead baby in the room and begging to be moved, her pleas coming out as barely comprehensible moans. Her cornrows were long overdue for rebraiding, and her traditional wrap was faded at each fold—a sure sign that it had been creased in the same way for days. Her hands are always clammy and cold, and her eyes—oh, those eyes! They grab you with their size and then scare you with their yellow tint.

Josephine arrived at the hospital in a wheelbarrow with an infected, open, ankle fracture. Her ankle had been broken weeks earlier and left uncared for. Her good ankle is thin, but this one is swollen with fluid, and a mess of infection sits around the broken bone.

She leans toward the reeking foot at all times; I doubt that she ever really turns her attention from that foot during the day. She often says things she doesn't mean and swings into fits during the late hours of the night.

Sometimes, it seems that she's *mentally* troubled. Other times, it's clear that she has a lot of *life* trouble. And still other times, I'm certain she's out to *make* trouble for the nursing staff. Underneath her head wrap, her cornrows, her skin, and her tough skull, there are layers upon layers of complicated brain matter.

The dead baby was two hours deceased, two days old, and had been born an unfortunate two months too early. The mother had begged that I let her keep the wrapped-up bundle in bed with her until morning. I half didn't know what to do and half felt sympathy toward her—so I agreed.

Obviously upset, Josephine glanced at the baby repeatedly and then pleaded to be moved farther away. No other beds were open, the one she was in was across the room, just about as far from the baby as possible, and I had no one to help me move her anyway.

When Josephine couldn't stand it any longer, she—twitching all the while—climbed out of her bed in a nervous rush, completely convinced that she had no other option. She thought that if she stayed in that bed a moment longer, she'd be attacked by the spirits of the dead. Not being able to walk, she scooted herself along the dirty hospital floor, waving her infected foot in the air. She scooted and moaned, scooted and moaned, and her bony, uninfected foot made a clean line in the floor as she hauled herself down the hall. She curled up on the cement in the maternity ward and fell asleep until morning.

selfish

I walked out of my hut and sat on the big root of our central tree while I drank *bouiller* (pronounced like *we* with a *b* in front of it: *bwe*). Bouiller is made from rice flour—rice that has been pounded to into a dusty powder. The rice flour and water are boiled together. Jolie sometimes adds goat's milk, sugar, and maybe lime. It's a Chadian comfort food, something you give to the sick and to children. When they give me bouiller, they always give me SO much—maybe a whole quart or more. No one else gets as much as I do. I always try to get someone to come and drink some of mine, but they always quickly and forcefully decline, saying, "No, Emily. You need to eat all of it!"

They taught me the word for "selfish" in Nangjere the other day. It's pronounced *"lee-seen-ya."* Now that I know this word, they use it all the time. Right after they bring me my huge bowl, they say, "Oh, Emily is *soooooo* selfish." I quickly fight back, "No! I'm not selfish! Here, eat some!" I beg them, shoving the bowl toward each of them. But everyone says, "No, no! We know you are selfish. We can't eat any of your bouiller," and they laugh hard. They frame me every time! There I am, with my big bowl all to myself—looking truly *lee-seen-ya.*

Another phrase that has become a wonderful source of laughter sounds like this: *"Gba. Tuckla duja!"* It means, "Come. Fight me!" Lanky fifteen-year-old Mounden puts up his sticklike arms and challenges me with this phrase. If I can keep from dying of laughter, I put up my fists and tell him he doesn't know what's coming. I tell him that I know he's afraid of me and then I rub his head with my knuckles. When the kids see us wrestling, they come running, bringing their sharp little fists. *"Gba. Tuckla duja!"* There's so much love in this house.

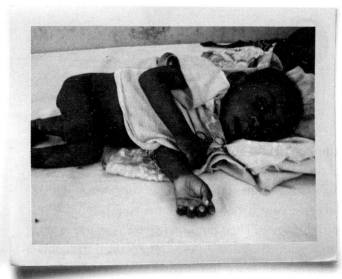

A malnourished child lies alone on a plastic mattress in his own diarrhea.

bones angling

I'm looking at a two-year-old boy who was just diagnosed with TB. He's been sitting for hours on his bed cross-legged, bones angling out all over the place—from his shoulders and knees and ribs and spine. I want to give him food, but he isn't hungry. He barely moves his sad eyes and doesn't cry. I think he must know that crying takes energy, and he doesn't have any to spare. He doesn't lie down—doesn't want to sleep.

out of orbit

The days that I think about heaven, I feel hopeful for those who suffer and less anxious about all the unrest. I'm thinking about this because today I saw a woman with cancer the size of a basketball in her stomach. Her mat is worn where she has survived on it—surviving for who knows how much longer or in how much more pain. It seems no matter how many blankets get thrown around the shoulders of the homeless and how many dollars are given to charity, this spinning world is out of orbit, that perfect orbit—and it will be until it's made new.

Lord, please make it new soon.

Part Five

Give

Neither Jolie nor Samedi have asked me to give them anything during my time here. Nothing. This is something really incredible for this culture. It's made me feel they really respect me.

Other people ask me for things all the time. "Give me your shirt." "Give me your water bottle." "Give me your banana." "Give me your hair."

The little kids like to ask for toys, balloons, or pencils. I've made it my goal to teach them that asking for things isn't polite. I explain it to them, saying, "I want to be your friend, but when the only thing you say to me is 'Give me this, give me that,' I just don't feel like I'm a friend."

The other day I gave my speech to a small group of children and a light-bulb went on in the head of one adorable little boy. He said, "Oh! Yes, yes!" and nodded enthusiastically. Then, looking very serious, he said to all the other kids, "We shouldn't ask for things," and with that, grabbed my hand.

I was at the market recently and purchased a bag of dried figs. When I eat them, I feel like I'm eating fresh produce, and it's almost enough to trick myself into feeling healthy. These figs have seeds in the middle, but the outer layer is like fruit leather—fruit leather and tiny bugs, which I eat and don't think about because I want to eat the figs so badly.

As I was snacking on these figs on the walk home, I passed a woman carrying a huge bowl of rice on her head. She said, "Give me some!" so I reached in and gave her a small handful of figs. Then, motioning toward her rice bowl, I said, "You give *me* some!" Without a second thought and with a very serious face, she reached up, took out a handful of rice kernels, and poured them into my palms. I was half kidding with her, but she took me seriously and looked rather pleased with herself!

Maybe they're trying to say something when they ask for something, such as, "Show me we are friends, give me something of yourself." Every time I give without a second thought, I make a new friend. And what does it cost me to give after all? A few less figs to eat.

It's easy to be defensive and paranoid about people taking advantage of you. Sometimes I feel stingy. And when I think about Jesus' challenge to live differently, my thought processes go something like this:

"Love your enemies." OK. That's vague enough. I think I can do that.

"Do good to those who hate you" [Matthew 5:44, NKJV]. *All right, it's not like He defines good—not a problem.*

"Pray for the happiness of those who curse you. Pray for those who hurt you" [Luke 6:28, NLT]. *Yeah, OK, He's just asking for words—totally doable.*

"If someone strikes you, stand there and take it. If someone drags you into court and sues for the shirt off your back, giftwrap your best coat and make a present of it. And if someone takes unfair advantage of you, use the occasion to practice the servant life. No more tit-for-tat stuff. Live generously" [Luke 6:29, 30, *The Message*]. *Whoooaaa! That's kind of a bigger deal.*

These verses leave me speechless because they are hard to get around, and they straight up call me to live in a different way than I do. Give what I have to anyone who asks for it? He couldn't really have meant that literally, we tell ourselves. But inside of me, it's both nerve racking and exciting when I think He just might have, because I honestly wonder what it would be like to live with such a free and giving attitude—and I wonder what the outcome might be. What if we run out of food? What if we give everything we have? What if the fish and bread *don't* multiply?

I'm attached to a lot of things. Certain clothes, certain books, certain times of the day. I grip them tightly and hide them behind my back because giving *them* away would be hard. And I tell myself, "Come on, Em—loosen the grip."

soap

I was washing my laundry at the well the other day, and when I finished, a couple of the boys came over. They picked up my wet and half-used Holiday Inn soap bars and said they liked them. I told them they could have them, and when I did, the older boy immediately snatched the bar of soap the other boy was holding and gave him the bar he'd had, which was smaller.

This irritated me. I said, "Hey, why did you do that? That soap was his." He said, "He's younger; he gets the smaller one." I argued for a bit with the older boy, telling him, "It's better when you give the bigger thing to the other person and take the smaller one for yourself." He just kept shaking his head.

So, thinking I'd teach him a lesson, I pulled out a brand-new bar of soap and gave it to the littler boy. The older boy instantly started reaching for the brand-new bar of soap! I said, "NO! That is for him. I want to give this to him." Finally, I used the word *selfish, "lee-seen-ya,"* and he got the hint.

skin and bones and teeth and eyes

I gave a shot IM (intramuscular) today, and there was no M on the little boy. I hate malnutrition. Strong word, I know.

He lies there, his existence put in question by his diminishing mass. I ask myself, *How? How does a three-year-old come to have ankles the size of my thumbs before the parents see that he's sick?* The child vomits up everything that goes into his stomach, and this nausea has killed his interest in food, increasing the problem.

A mother tries to feed porridge to her malnourished child who resists her efforts.

As the mother held the baby against her, she took his arm and straightened it, revealing his little antecubital. I ran my finger along his loose skin, searching for a vein to target. I wrapped the tourniquet twice around the place where a bicep should be, and the small bit of tension I applied seemed like it threatened to snap his bone. The skin folded back on itself, twisting and finding itself pinched by the rubber's grip. How loose those folds were—and how far they stretched away from the baby's frame, reminding me that his body was never meant to be this small.

I keep reminding the little boy's mother that she needs to wash his clothes—wash the drape that she is wrapping him in. I say, "Take off this shirt, there's vomit on it. Get him a different one." The father pauses, thinks for a bit, and then says, "We don't have another one." *Ah, you're an idiot, Emily,* I think. Blinking long and hard and taking a deep breath, I remember that it's not like they wanted this for their baby; somehow they've just found themselves here.

The baby doesn't move but begins to pee on his mother's dress. Neither she nor he will have their clothes washed anytime soon. After their clothing dries, they'll smell like stale urine but will have to endure it.

When the IVs are all dripping quinine, vitamins, antibiotics, and glucose, and I have time, I let myself be unrealistic. I think about all the people that I could give these babies to back home. I'd buckle them into airplane seats and send them to families who would be waiting with strollers and pacifiers. This one could go to the Davises. This one could be raised by my grandparents. I'll bet Carley Brown would take this one, and he'd be a cyclist someday. These friends and family members of mine could nurse the children back to health.

But the cries of one of the babes brings me back to reality—back to the situation as it is. I know we can't change the world by moving every human out of the bad parts and into the good parts. We have to try to make the bad parts good. And really, where is it truly good already anyway?

Oh, but sometimes it's overwhelming. I want to put these babies in a bed with covers. I want them to sleep in a room that doesn't smell so bad, and I want them to eat food that contains vitamins.

Sometimes I realize that the depression that is coming into my accounts of my experiences in Chad reveals what is starting to coat my eyes. The suffering I see every day is all I've been able to focus on lately. I've got to peel all that back, because honestly, there is plenty of joy flooding the hours of the day. I determine to try to write about something happier next time.

My boyfriend, Alex, wrote an e-mail to me. In it he said he had read recently that reality can be changed by our perceptions! When we see something as good, we make it better. I believe it. There's a song by Relient K that I listened to today. It's old, but it speaks about the very thing that I've been experiencing lately. All these things are just building up and sometimes it's hard to start a day feeling optimistic. But the last line of this song says, "Today, I'll trust you [Lord] with the confidence of a man who's never known defeat."

Yes. The confidence of a man who's never known defeat. My courage and confidence are waning and need to be reassessed.

dance your heart out

At night, in the light of a fire, everything becomes more beautiful. The shadows and lights, brights and darks, are almost as pretty as the colors we enjoy during the day.

Last night while I was finishing my porridge, Crispen, Tony, and Pabris were throwing their bodies all over the grass mat, fidgeting, poking me, and nibbling at peanuts. Their attempt at relaxing seemed tainted by or perhaps was even a result of boredom.

Then Jolie came out of her hut and walked toward the fire, choosing a spot across from me. She pressed her hands together at chest height, began to move her shoulders rhythmically in circles, and sang Nangjere chants, humming when she forgot the words. Eventually, she added native dances to her performance. The fire was casting her shadow up on the mud wall, and the kids giggled and then rolled with laughter as they watched the shadow's portrayal of their grandmother's dances.

Their laughter added fuel to the fire within Jolie. She stopped her dancing, told everyone to wait right where we were, and went into her hut. When she emerged, her skirt was tied up between her legs to form makeshift pants, and she had tied a strip of cloth around her forehead and left the ends dangling. Her new costume seemed to make her all the more animated—she did kicks with her feet, performed warrior dances with the three young boys, and made me laugh hysterically, which meant Encore! Encore!

Jolie is the source of so much of my joy here—and not just my joy, but that of our whole family. I want to be more like Jolie. Her joy is contagious. I hope I catch it.

attention

I remember when I ran away from home at the age of eight. I went out to the forest back of our house and sat in the pine needles, thinking that someone would notice that I was gone and send a search party.

I sat for what seemed to be a long time. I didn't like being alone or sitting where I had to sweep ants off of my legs and where all sorts of pinecones and pine needles poked me in the rear. But I thought the attention I would get was going to make the discomfort worth it. *Oh, the moment when they find me and feel awful for not bending to my every whim before!* I thought, *They'll wish they had paid more attention to me!*

I also remember being a kid and getting in one of those really obnoxious moods in which I hassled my uncle endlessly. He kept me at arm's length, playfully pushing me away while continuing whatever adult conversation he was in. It was obvious that I was asking for something, and finally, I just plain demanded it. I yelled, "GIVE ME ATTENTION!"

African children soak up attention like sponges. I've never seen kids so hungry for it. Little Armelle will, out of nowhere, yell out the word *yellow* just because she knows it's English and that I'll look toward her. Pabris will roll in the dirt just so people will gasp at his lack of inhibition. Aaron will call my name and then, realizing he has nothing to say, he'll make some crazy face just to get a reaction. The kids bring their homework and set it in my lap, balance pots on their heads, pretend they are going to eat frogs, and point to their new clothes—anything to get attention.

It seems as we get older we learn to live with less attention. Or perhaps, as we grow older, the world demands so attention from us that we just want to escape from its eye. Whatever the case, these kids are still soaking up attention.

letting go of the reins

Yikes! Stephan, Ansley, and I raced the three horses tonight. It raised the *exact* same feeling that I have when I drive in the fog back in the States—that of tossing caution slightly into the wind. No matter how slow you go, you don't know what will come out of the fog. It's a risky, edgy feeling—one I felt while riding this horse. We were flying! I usually hold the reins tight and keep the horse steady at some speed, but tonight I just let the reins go.

It was beautiful! I felt the bit of energy normally suppressed by the tension in the reins surge into the horse's legs. My only concern was that the horse I was riding is extremely skittish—and just about anything can set him off. He sees a bush and jumps to the side. He hears a baby cry and he jumps to the side. He passes under a tree and he jumps to the side. So you have to be ready!

I felt like a good person for letting him run free. It felt like the right thing to do for a horse. I also felt like I was pushing my luck. Falling off at those speeds could result in broken bones or things being dislocated. I leaned back on the reins for all I was worth, and we came to a stop by a grove of trees. The sun had left us, so we turned around and took the trail home, arriving at the stable after dark. We pulled the sweaty saddles and blankets off of the panting horses and put them away.

contentment

I handed baby Galas to Cecil at 11 P.M. and got up to walk to my hut. I could hear noise coming from the street in front of my house, something that sounded like teenagers—boys and girls flirting maybe. First, there'd be one voice telling a joke, followed by a lot of laughter, next bursts of conversation between many pairs, and then someone saying something to the group as a whole. They were socializing.

I swung my hut door open and walked blindly into my pitch-black hut. I shuffled my feet along the dirt floor until my shins hit the cot, at which point I collapsed into bed. I waited for the thoughts of home and feelings that I was a misfit to set in as had happened on so many other nights, but they never came. I felt OK. I even felt lucky. I felt the early symptoms of contentment.

My settled body asked my unusually settled mind, *Is this what you have been wishing for? Is this the beginning of the state of mind you envisioned sinking into?* I couldn't ask for an answer because the only answer I can trust is the permanent feeling of contented belonging residing within me. Time will tell.

handle that

I really don't think I can do this. I'm NOT a nurse. I feel like a second-grader on move-up day, during which, for one day, you get to try out being a third-grader. They give you division and multiplication problems and ask you to write haiku poems—things you've never done before. Inside your little, challenged mind you think, *Oh, I want the teacher to like me! I want to succeed here. I want to be able to be a third-grader, but I don't think I can.*

Last night I worked the night shift. Maybe they should call it the "eternity-long shift," because it goes from 3 P.M. to 8 A.M. I was scheduled to work with an incredibly knowledgeable and levelheaded Chadian nurse named Augustan, but when I arrived, he was terribly sick with malaria. I don't think he got rid of it the last time he had it. Last night he was vomiting and shaking with chills when he told me he couldn't work. Scared at the likely implications of what he said, I begged him not to go home. I can't be the only staff on duty at the hospital, I need someone whom I can ask medical dosage questions, someone to receive emergency patients, someone with knowledge and confidence—two things I felt I was lacking. I told Augustan he could sleep and wouldn't have to lift a finger, "But please," I said, "don't leave me alone!"

He climbed onto the maternity table in the delivery room, and I gave him my blanket, which he tucked under his shivering body all around. Still, as I left the room and shut the door behind me, I stood in the hall thinking, *I really don't think I can do this. The wards are full right now because after the rice season everyone feels rich, and they're all coming to get long-overdue treatment for their health problems.*

Isolation ward: Completely full.
Maternity: No room left.
Pediatrics: Not a bed open.
Women's ward: Overflowing.
Men's ward: Surgery patience galore.

I had come at three o'clock, thinking in the evening I'd have a break during which I could run home, get my headlamp, and eat a quick bite of something supperish. But I never left the hospital.

That child's blood transfusion clotted off. This baby needs diazepam because he's convulsing. This other baby's IV is so infiltrated that the baby has a massive balloon of water under his skin. I need to start the IV for the woman in the emergency room, give the six o'clock meds, and take the temperatures of any critical babies. That's all there's time for now. Then I have to run back and forth between wards and give nine o'clock meds. So I never went home.

Knowing I hadn't been able to make it home, Dinga and Esther came to the hospital at nine thirty with a tray holding a cute little pot of oil-soaked pasta, covered with a hand-crocheted doily to keep some heat in. I have sweet sisters.

About 10:30 P.M. I thought I might fail. I thought I wasn't capable of doing everything that needed to be done. I hit rock bottom. I've decided that was the best thing that could have happened to me right then. When you bounce a basketball on hard ground, it bounces back. If you don't hit hard, you'll just drag the rest of the night. That night I had a good little session of prayer, stargazing, and remembering that time after time all these things turn out OK; and I said to myself, "Buck up, Emily. Tough it out!"

The night was still long. I had a million meds to give between eleven and one. But at 1:30 A.M., I was able to take care of everything I needed to. Then I lay down on a skinny cement bench outside of the emergency room. The bench fits between my shoulder blades, which keeps me from rolling off to either side.

I can never wait for the sun to come back in the morning. There's a loneliness that haunts the night shifts. The patients who sleep at night sleep hard. The patients who don't sleep are crying or else are in so much pain that they just sit or lie in bed in silence. That's eerie and leaves me anxious.

At 4:30 A.M., I went around and gave all the 5 A.M. meds. Still pitch black. The battery from my phone was running low from substituting as a flashlight all night long. But the sun crept up, and a wash of peace came over me. I had told myself I would praise God with everything inside me when I saw the morning light. I look back on it now and realize I shouldn't have waited. I should have been thankful at 10:30 P.M. At rock bottom. Because rock bottom is what sends us up. Rock bottom makes us different people—stronger, more God-dependent people. I'm pretty sure Augustan needs IV fluids now. There's no way he has any fluid left in him.

collision

Jolie seems to be very, very perceptive. Sometimes when we're around the fire at night, I let my eyes glaze over. When I do, they can see only blurry dots in the sky and make out only an orange glow where the coals are burning down. While my eyes are resting, my brain isn't, and the thinking it's doing is uncontrolled and zoned out. It's easy for me to fall into this situation because I don't understand enough Nangjere to follow the fast-paced conversations of the rest of my family.

Jolie will catch me zoning and ask with a sweet smile, "Emily, what are you thinking about? Are you thinking about Alice?" Then Esther, embarrassed, snaps at her mother, "Every time, Mama!" It's true; Jolie can't pronounce Alex's name, and the name *Alice* has become the funny substitute.

Jolie asks me if I've gotten a letter from him lately and if he's coming to visit. Her questions go deeper, and she asks me if we'll marry. I backpedal. If you've ever done that on a bike, you know it takes you nowhere. So, I'm forced to move forward and explain. "I'll finish my education, get to know him more, and then maybe, we will see." I tell her it will be years. She disagrees and tells me, No, I will have children soon. Because she's so certain and I can tell the thought brings her great joy, I just laugh and don't argue.

Then she asks me if I'm thinking about my family. She asks how they are doing and if they are healthy. I ask for the lamp, run to my hut, and bring back a set of pictures. As I go through them, she can't tell the difference between my mother and me—much like I couldn't tell the difference between my African siblings for quite some time. Jolie handles the pictures with such care, as if they're the people themselves. The children question me about the pictures until I'm tired, because my family back home is so different from them. They imitate the funny faces that my friends are making in some of the pictures and hold the pictures up so people can compare their imitations to the originals. Each of them is trying to relate to and enjoy the things they've never seen.

Sometimes I imagine my parents shaking hands with my African parents here in Béré. I imagine the things they'd have in common. Jolie would show my mom the fabrics that she sells every day at the market. They would pore over them and match colors or choose their favorite patterns. My dad would go over to the hospital with Samedi, and they might assess patients together or assist each other in procedures.

Then I imagine them meeting at my home in America. Jolie would do the dishes with my mom, and my mom would teach her about the dishwasher. That would be strange, for sure. My dad would take Samedi out to our barn, show him our motorbike, and let him take it for a spin. Samedi would ride all over our mountain and probably stall the engine because Chad is flat and he's never used a clutch on hills.

I imagine the meeting of these two worlds producing a collision of sorts, and something happening as a result—a whole lot of learning for sure, but something beyond that practical, factual learning. I imagine there would be a deeper understanding of humanity.

please let this be a silent night

Baby born without a hole between his nasal canal and throat.
Dr. Appel made one.
Baby is doing great thanks to awesome, dedicated parents.

Cerebral malaria coma patient woke up tonight!
Comas scare me.
He's only twenty.

Eighteen-year-old boy with meningitis.
He will recover.

Ten-year-old boy with meningitis.
I honestly don't know if he'll make it.
He's so frail, and his muscles have contracted so far already.

Young girl with nephritic syndrome.
Her whole body is holding water, and I'm afraid she'll die.
The last girl with this same problem died right in front of me.

Josephine said things were *"Lapia"*—Good!
She seemed to be in good spirits and didn't wail tonight.
Her foot is still very infected.
We're changing the dressing twice a day now.

Sweet little man caring for his wife.
She has malaria.
He is the best little husband.

Another woman with malaria.
It's so bad I don't think she'll make it.
And the doctor says there's nothing more we can do for her.

Woman recovering from an emergency hysterectomy.
She's had no children yet.
Her husband will probably send her back to her father and take another
    wife.

Hippo bite.
Man was knocked out of his dugout and into the water by a hippo.
He escaped with only a big bite out of his leg.
Lucky.

Baby Adoum had a large part of the skin on his belly removed because
    of infection.
Changing his dressing makes me cringe.

This is only a tiny sampling of the people who are resting in this hospital tonight. I'm listening to "Silent Night" on my iPod now, and the words are echoing in this little cement nurses' station. I change them in my head to something like

Sleep in heavenly peace, babies.
Please sleep through the night.
All is calm and all is bright, Josephine,
Please let your mind rest for tonight.

Three hours later.
I prayed for this to be a silent night, but I just got back from carrying a woman to the morgue. She was the one who had the really aggressive malaria.
What a helpless feeling when all you can do isn't enough. This woman was seventy. She was the oldest patient I've seen yet. Her family will come and get her in the morning. This is the first time I've actually been in the morgue. There is still blood on the floor from the massacre in October. Sometimes this place feels like a real nightmare.

a child was born

On the day before Christmas, I was huddled with a girl named Grace around a tiny wire basket. The basket holds about six really hot coals that send out a circle of heat. Grace and I surrounded the basket with our bodies and trapped all the heat we could between the two of us. I kept my eye on her skirt, anxiously anticipating that her close proximity to the fire will cause her clothes to light up and burns to mark her flesh. We've seen this quite often at the hospital, and I'm starting to worry like an old woman.

Sitting there, my mind wandered again, and I thought about Joseph leading Mary on their donkey (that must have been a very uncomfortable ride), knowing that Mary was feeling the birthing pains and needed to get to a place where she could have the baby. That rush to the hospital on a donkey during the night sounds familiar.

A mother came in the other day to have her baby, and there wasn't time to get her to the delivery room. She delivered right in the emergency room. The trash can was placed under her to catch all the fluids.

The baby came out screaming as though he'd been breathing air all nine months in there. Augustan handed me the wet little bundle, and Hortance and I ran over to the maternity ward, where we could rub him up, tie off his cord, put some protective cream in his eyes, and take all his measurements. Babies can come so fast.

I'll bet Joseph felt a lot of responsibility for Mary. I'll bet he was afraid that the baby would come while Mary was still on the donkey—while they were still traveling.

Another man came into our hospital with his wife and for some reason didn't go to the emergency room, where we usually assess new patients, but instead came to the medical-surgical ward where I was working. He said, "Please, madame, my wife is about to give birth," and he motioned to her, round bellied and exhausted. The maternity ward room was locked, so we laid her down on a bed meant for post-maternity patients.

Because I don't exactly know a ton about obstetrics and I don't exactly have ANY training in midwifery, I always think the baby is going to come in the first three minutes after the expectant woman arrives at the hospital, and so I hurry around frantically, calling the midwife, finding the key, and getting the things ready. Then the baby doesn't come for another six hours.

The husband was quite worried about his wife, which was sweet and made me want to be married. She delivered a few hours later just fine. A curly headed little boy.

Mary must have been scared—this was her first baby, and first births are hard. I'll bet Jesus' birth was painful, and I'll bet Mary wondered, *Why in the world did I agree to this?*

And Jesus' birth—what a crazy story for us nowadays in America. But people are still giving birth in mud huts here in Africa. Mothers still arrive at this hospital on donkeys and ask for a place to have their baby. I'm excited about tomorrow. Christmas is bound to bring joy.

tinsel

It was Christmas Eve. I fell asleep on a mattress to the sound of all the foreign volunteers singing Christmas carols at the house of the mission pilot and his wife, Gary and Wendy Roberts. Maybe an hour later, I woke up extremely homesick. Gary gave three of us girls a ride to our village. (That means four were on the moto!)

I had no idea how to shake my homesickness on Christmas Eve, so I just sulked back to my family's huts. When I got there, Jolie was sitting by the coals with two of her cousins. I went over and sat down with them, and she introduced me, settling me into the warm and peaceful atmosphere of their company. The conversation went from America to marriage to my not showering that morning, to what it would be like for my African family to visit me in America, to Mounden, who was clanking pots together as he searched for food in the dish hut. He'd missed supper, and so now he was incredibly hungry.

I tried to make room for him to sit with us, but Jolie said, "No! He's a boy!" So he sat at the edge of the circle of ladies. Eventually, however, he ended up in the circle with us. We were all crowded so close, touching shoulders as we hovered over the coals, and every time something was really funny, Jolie, shouldering me at the right, would place one hand on my leg, the other arm around my shoulders, and throw back her head in laughter. I felt so loved there that my homesickness began to lift.

The previous weekend I had gone went to Moundou—a city about three hours away. Jolie told me that she kept thinking about me that weekend, and when she wanted to talk to me, I wasn't there. Then she told me that when I leave for America, she would lose a daughter.

"Ma fille," she called me. My daughter.

Oh, I just love her. How could I feel this much love for a group of people in such a short time?

Christmas morning I woke up early and finished putting the tags on the tiny presents that I'd prepared for each member of the family. The kids started hobbling out around 6:30, their little shoulders were caved forward as they held their hands between their thighs, trying to keep warm. It was such a funny sight—all these freezing African kids with their hands between their legs. So I brought out all my scrub tops and some of my other shirts, and the kids pulled them on for warmth. We looked like a child-Chadian-operating-room team.

Then I brought out all the paper snowflakes that we had made the day before and hung them on our mango tree. (Actually, I made most of the snowflakes—these kids haven't learned how to use scissors yet.) The branches of the tree are like a canopy, so imagine all the snowflakes hanging at head level. Then we strung tinsel and ribbon all over. The decorating we did felt different than the decorating I did at home, but somehow it still had a familiar feel! After all, *it was Christmas*!

By the time we finished decorating, the neighborhood had gathered around us. I realized that if my family were to open presents under the tree, there would be lots of disappointed people who didn't get presents. We had to wait for Samedi to come home from working the night shift anyway, so I went into the girls' hut, where Esther and Dinga were resting on mats. When Samedi arrived, he came into the hut where we were and I told him our problem. "Samedi," I said, "I have little gifts for everyone in our family, but I don't have enough for all the neighbors out there. I feel bad!" He said, "Oh, don't feel bad, Emily. We can all come in here—just the family. I'll get everyone." So all nineteen of us piled into one little mud hut.

I told them what Christmas meant to me (in pretty chopped-up French), and Samedi translated into Nangjere. They listened so quietly. Then I started handing them little gifts that had their names on them. I had anticipated that it wouldn't be that enjoyable because I thought it would be like me giving handouts (which I detest), and all the kids would scramble for the gifts they wanted. However, I think because each gift had a specific name on it, they didn't envy each other's gifts. They gave me many sweet, sweet Thank yous—and people rarely say "Please" and "Thank you" here. I've never had so much fun giving.

I gave Samedi one of those pack lights, which he loves. It's the brightest light he's ever owned. Mounden got an intricate mechanical music box—

only the inside moving parts—and he couldn't stop winding it up and watching it, trying to figure out how it worked. Dinga got Floam—that moldable putty made out of tiny foam balls. No one knew what it was, and at one point I saw that they were all tasting it! It looks and feels exactly like that big ball of rice called *boule* that we eat every day! By the time I said, "NO! Don't eat it!" the taste had told them it wasn't edible.

It was a festive Christmas, meaningful and family filled—but I missed my family in America a lot. I thought a lot about toasty fireplaces and drifts of snow. I thought about the music that's playing constantly and my dad always smelling like gasoline because he's always driving the snowmobile around. I'm missing everyone a lot! I keep reminding myself that the anticipation of reunions only builds with time and that makes them even more wonderful when they actually arrive. Be patient, Emily. Be present, Emily.

Horse Riding

I used to look at clothes here in Chad and wonder how in the world did they get so many holes in them? I thought the clothes must be ancient! There were holes everywhere—not just in places like the neckline or armpits, where you would expect them, but there were holes in the middle of the chest—and lots of them! But now that I've been here for four months, my clothes are starting to get holes in them too. Just the other day, little Armelle stuck her finger through a hole in the knee of my jeans. Wear and tear. Chad deals roughly with everything; including me lately.

The last two weeks have been especially and increasingly difficult. I've found myself spending more time away from the hospital. I used to stay late and help with deliveries and observe sur-

Far too late to think of steering Libby in another direction, I saw a huge branch rapidly approaching.

geries, but now I find myself looking forward to the end of my shift and becoming frustrated if the next nurse is even a little bit late. After yesterday's shift, which sucked my optimism dry, Stephan and I decided to go riding. The horses seem to calm us and free us from the frustrations we feel.

We rode through the village and out the east exit, and little kids ran as fast as they could alongside the horses, trying to keep up. One little boy ran out from his hut and immediately began doing the horse skip—you know, the one little kids do—and making *clippity-clop* sounds as his feet threw up puffs of dust.

The branches of the mango trees hung low as we rode, demanding that you either duck really low and dodge them or close your eyes and turn your head so you protect your eyes as you slide through them. Before mango season came, the closing-your-eyes method worked wonderfully. The branches were full of leaves that just brushed over your body. However, now there are hard green, unripe mangoes hidden in the leaves, and as Libby, the horse I was riding, took me straight through the trees, that fact became apparent to me, and I had a little moment of panic as my upper body passed through the leaves. I was just *expecting* a hidden mango to hit me right in the face or something. Miraculously, I went through the whole batch of branches and didn't hit a single one.

My mind was so occupied with thoughts of my invincibility that the next tree caught me off guard. Far too late to think of steering Libby in another direction, I saw a huge branch rapidly approaching, and this one was not simply composed of leaves—at its center was a thick, solid hunk of wood. Just in time I threw myself forward onto Libby's spiny neck while grasping at her thin mane. Both Libby and I BARELY made it under the branch! SO CLOSE! I laughed out loud—a bit out of shock and a bit out of the feeling that I was an idiot, that it's only in movies that people get knocked off their horses by branches. But it wasn't entirely funny. I could have been seriously injured.

appetite

When you're a baby, you eat your fingers as if they taste good. And babies keep going back for more! Baby Goma eats dirty, unripe green mangoes here—ones that have been dropped in the dirt multiple times. Goma will chew on them all day long, and I doubt he likes the taste.

We develop appetites for hundreds of things—for style and foods, for boyfriends and art, to name four—yet sometimes we forget to *taste* the things we've begun to crave. Do I like the things I do? Do the fingers really taste good, or am I shoving my fist in my mouth out of habit? Am I eating the things I like or am I passively gnawing at green mangoes?

Velcro

This morning I am twenty-three.

I came home last night after a sweet birthday celebration at Wendy and Gary's that included puffy chocolate cake. When I got home, Dinga and Esther were sitting outside where the teenagers talk at night. I sat down with them in the dark, and they teased me, saying I must have an African boyfriend whom I visit at night and that they were going to tell Alex. Esther said that when she told Alex, he would want her and he'd be her boyfriend. This joke never gets old. We can joke about boyfriends every day and always think it's funny.

After some good laughs with these funny African sisters, I unlocked my tin door and started getting settled for bed. When I began to get into bed, I realized that I had done laundry earlier in the day and that my sheets and blanket were still hanging on a clothesline over at the hospital.

Super. No sheets. No blanket.

But I was much too tired to walk over and get them. And the sticky, hot evening air tricked me into thinking that it would be hot all night long. I was wearing my tasseled Indian capris, and my ankles began telling me to cover them. I grabbed the Santa outfit that my mom had sent at Christmas and wrapped it around my feet. Naively, I hoped I'd sleep all through the night without any blankets.

Wrong.

I woke up freezing.

Really freezing.

I pulled my arms inside the body portion of my shirt and tucked the sleeves behind my back so no drafts would come in. Trying not to think about the cold, I somehow made it to the morning. I got up and thought, *Emily, that was a rough night. But hey—you're twenty-three!*

I went outside and looked around. From the position of the sun, I judged that it was about seven in the morning. So I shuffled my way back into my hut, grabbed my running shoes, and I banged them on the ground

85

to get all the scorpions out. (OK, so none have ever fallen out, but I *have* seen scorpions in my room, and I can just imagine how much it would hurt if one stung my toe.) I sat down in my doorway to pull them on, and then I brushed my teeth. As I was putting my toothbrush away, my eyes caught sight of a bunch of the shoes that I still hadn't given out.

Lots of people from my hometown sent shoes for our little neighborhood running team, and it has been SO fun slowly distributing them to kids who I know are going to use them. I want to tell you my thought process about the shoes right now. I'm a little ashamed of it, but I think it's valuable to tell—so don't think less of me.

I got shoes of all kinds in the mail. I got Nike, Polo Sport, Keds, new and used and all different. Amazing! Two of the pairs of shoes had Velcro instead of laces and looked like they were for the elderly. They were navy blue with fairly thick foamlike heels; comfortable, but not sporty. I didn't know who to give those to because I thought all the kids would want the nice, new running shoes and I thought they'd get upset if they were the ones who got an old-school Velcro pair. (I had forgotten the appreciative and content attitude that Africans have.)

I thought of my dad. He's hip in his own way. Perhaps it's the way he sports colors from a different decade that is so intriguing, or maybe it's the way he tosses into the wind all thought of pleasing the fashion industry. He wears things that are absolutely outdated, and we laugh at him because his light-blue work jacket is SO tattered, our cross-country ski set is from the seventies, and our biking helmets are shaped like mushrooms—ancient! But I love that about both of my parents. Life isn't about having the nicest things. People will always have nicer things. So this is why I'm a bit ashamed that I looked down on the blue Velcro shoes at all.

Anyway, this morning when I saw the Velcro something clicked and I thought, *Kousimmia!*

Kousimmia led the pack the other evening. Barefoot runners. We were running little trails on the flat, dry rice fields when Kousimmia said, "We are all birds!" He threw an arm out to the side like a bird in flight, while in place of the other arm, long ago amputated, a knob flapped under his shirt sleeve. Everyone followed his lead, and for the next three minutes straight, we flapped our arms, and we WERE like a stream of geese flying south. These kids didn't even THINK about how silly we looked. They loved it! So did I.

One-winged birds are something amazing. This was the first time I had seen one.

Kousimmia is a flier, even with just one arm.

The kids make fun of him sometimes. Some bully will shake an arm around behind his body as if it is detached or another will laugh when he misses a shot in basketball. But Kousimmia seems to just shake it all off. He's learned so much basketball. He runs. He's learning English really well. He just flies!

But Kousimmia wanted shoes. He's been running without them, but I could tell he wanted them, and he frequently asked if any his size had come in. This morning, when I saw that pair of Velcro shoes, I thought, *This is the reason the Velcro shoes came!* Taking them in hand, I asked the other kids where Kousimmia lived. They directed me there, and I found his family standing around with their big bull, getting ready to take him to the fields. I stood at a distance because if this beast simply nodded his head in the wrong direction, he could put a hole in me with his horns. The littlest boy held the threat on a rope, and I asked him if he wasn't even a little bit scared. He said, "No," and hugged this massive animal from under his belly. This kid is fearless!

I told Kousimmia that I had some shoes for him, and his crooked smile just shot forth. I strapped the shoes on him, and they fit perfectly. HE LOVED THEM! Lace-up shoes just wouldn't work for him because he can't tie them with only one hand.

I said, "You wanna go now?"

"Yes!"

So we went. Koomakung, the fearless six-year-old, came with us. He has incredible endurance—he didn't stop once. I couldn't believe it. It was such a good birthday run.

I hadn't seen the value in those Velcro shoes. It seems I've got in my head that we have to have the best. But today, on my birthday, I found that something was better than the best. I'm so thankful for those who sent the shoes. Especially the pair of Velcro shoes. I'll never think badly of Velcro again. I promise.

housekeeping

After I finished my *bouiller*, I saw Jago and David cleaning out their hut and I decided that my hut needed a deep cleaning too. All the kids wanted to help me, and that was fine with me—I'm all about cleaning in groups; it's so much more fun. I once told Fletcher (my tidy younger brother) that I would help him clean his room if he would help me clean mine. His response provoked feelings of both irritation and love. He said, "Emily, that's like Mexico telling the U.S., hey, we'll help you with your health care system if you help us with ours." *Grrr!* Anyway, my African siblings all came to my aid in this endeavor to deep clean my mud hut. *Hmmm.*

When I moved my teal suitcase, four big, drowsy, dehydrated frogs came hopping out, and all the kids wailed and pranced around, hugging the walls of the hut. No one wanted to touch them. Eventually, we made Tony push them out of the hut with his flip-flop. Then we moved my other suitcase and found that ants had burrowed into the ground, leaving mounds of dusty dirt. I began sweeping at these dirt piles with my hand broom—a stiff bundle of rice stalks chopped off evenly at the end and tied around the middle with a piece of fabric.

As I swept, dust started rising. Dinga grabbed the rice stalks from me, shaking her head and saying, *"Courra di"* (Not good). She sprinkled water all over the dirt floor, and then we could sweep the floor without threatening anyone with death by dust inhalation. I don't know why I never thought of this. Every time I tried to sweep, I could hardly breathe! Smarts—African street-smarts.

So, we swept the hut clean, and oh, it looked awesome! Then Izeedoor started flipping through the calendar that hangs on my wall, and as he did, a little scorpion scurried down to the floor. Not comforting! Izeedoor chased it down and smashed it with a wooden hammer. He was proud of himself, I could tell. I think all the frogs, ants, and scorpions are out now. I'll sleep so well tonight.

edgy

About nine o'clock last night, Carol, Ansley, and I were sitting together with the things we had brought for the night of adventure we were planning. Ansley had a backpack, headlamp, blanket, mattress, Nalgene bottle, toothbrush, toothpaste, candle with matches, and a snack. OK, she didn't really have a snack, but she had everything else.

Then there were Caroline and me. We seem to have similar theories on preparation—if you'll be OK without something, then you don't have to bring it. So if we can convince ourselves that we'll be OK trekking in the dark, then we don't bring a flashlight. If we can last till morning without a drink, we don't bring a water bottle. If we think we can tough the night out on hard ground without complaining, we don't bring a mattress. As you might guess, Caroline and I had packed a bit lighter than Ansley. We had the scrubs we were wearing and gum (which Caroline said we were bringing to ease our consciences since we weren't going to brush our teeth) and I had insisted that we take a blanket and sheet because I remembered the night I substituted a Santa suit for a blanket. Bad news!

We told Dr. Wilson (an awesome relief doctor from California) our plan: we wanted to spend the night on the flat top of the water tower. The hospital's water tower is a giant box on stilts; its top is about forty feet above the ground, and it has no guardrails; Dr. Wilson said he'd line the top with bricks to keep us from rolling off in our sleep, but we told him we'd be all right. I suggested that we tie our wrists together, but that didn't go over either.

Near the water tower, we found a twenty-foot-long metal ladder. Getting it to stand on end took all three of us, and even then it swayed all over the place—it would start leaning one way, so we'd push it until it was upright, but it would keep on going and nearly fall over the other way. We looked like those dumb robbers in comedies, trying to break into someone's house. But we got the ladder in place and climbed up it and then on up to the top of the water tower. The tank is capped by a semithin sheet of metal, our bed for the night. As we crawled across it, the metal kept flexing and making big booming sounds, which I knew everyone below could hear. I thought someone would say something and we'd be caught, but no one came outside to see what was going on.

We shifted around until we got semicomfortable and then lay there staring up at the black night and the stars. The tower was tall enough that being on top of it actually made us feel closer to the stars. We had an awesome conversation that night as we lay there. My dad says there's something about campfires and hot tubs that makes for great conversations. Maybe it's because they give you a reason to sit still for a while. Silences aren't awkward when you're sitting in a hot tub or by a campfire; when the conversation lags a bit you still have a reason to be there. I think I'm going to add stargazing to his theory. It seems to open people's minds and hearts and settles their nerves.

Eventually, everyone faded to unconsciousness—except me. It took me a long time. I've been having a hard time sleeping lately. My mind just won't turn off. Jolie says that if you think too much, you become skinny and sickly. Anytime she catches me daydreaming she tells me that if I get sickly, my family will say she didn't feed me enough. I want to make Jolie look good, but I have a lot to think about here too.

At 3 A.M., Caroline told me she was freezing and wasn't going to make it till morning, and she climbed down the tower and walked home. An hour later, Ansley said she was cold, too, and was going to leave. I begged her not to go right then. "Wait till it's a bit lighter," I said. "Then I'll go with you." So, she toughed it out.

When we climbed down from that tower, my body begged the sun to go back to wherever it was coming from and let me have a few more hours of sleep. But I've learned that a good sleep isn't usually part of a good adventure.

rice in the eye

When Fletcher, my younger brother, was four, he got a button stuck in his nose. He had shoved it so far in that removing it required a trip to the doctor, who had to use some special tool to reach in and pull it out. My mom sealed the button in a plastic pouch and taped it into his scrapbook so we'd never forget it, because these things are funny when you're in your twenties.

When I was fifteen—I'm embarrassed at how old I was—I somehow got a tiny mint stuck in my ear. I tried jumping up and down with my ear tilted toward the ground, but it didn't work. My mom took me to the doctor, and just as we were walking up the sidewalk to his office—I was still doing that jumping/shaking thing—the mint fell out.

It just happens—kids get things stuck in difficult places.

Today, a boy came into the emergency room accompanied by his father. The boy was holding his hand over his eye, and his father kept pushing it away so we could get a good look at it. The eye was swollen and leaking a little fluid out of the corner. The father had a swollen eye too; he explained that they had been working in the rice field the day before. It's harvest season for the rice, so the women, men, and children use their machete blades and shave the fields—big hard swings to hack down the stalks. In the process, some rice kernels fly free and apparently can be very hazardous to the eyes. These two had kernels of rice embedded deeply and painfully in the whites and pupils of their eyes. Believing that the kernels might work themselves out on their own, the two had waited a whole day before addressing the problem. Now, their eyes were irritated and puffy.

Dr. Francois tried to use his finger to scrape the rice out the boy's eye, but it was deeply situated, and the boy screamed and flailed. I held his arms and Job his legs, but the boy still made it impossible to extract the rice. It was obvious that unless he was unconscious, we couldn't help him, so Dr. Francois referred the two to a hospital far away, one where they had an apparatus to hold the head still.

Rice lodged in an eye. It's unlikely that you'd see that back home in the States, but it happens here in Chad.

twenty cents

Tonight, when it got late, Ongen, Jolie's daughter, who had been visiting for the evening, decided to head home. Merci, Esther, and I said we would accompany her across the village to her hut. I love that African tradition. As we walked, I tried to teach them to say in English, "Why are you laughing?" I wanted them to be able to say it with attitude when someone made fun of them for any reason (so I'm probably not teaching them the most useful English words). But they kept mispronouncing the line, saying something more like "Where is the bathroom?" So I just taught them that instead, having them say it back to me over and over again. Then I realized that I had three Africans repeatedly shouting, "Where is the bathroom?" as we walked through the village streets. I glanced around, wondering who else thought it was funny—but of course, no one else understood what Esther, Merci, and Ongen were saying.

Then they started shouting, "The bathroom is THAT way!" which they learned thanks to Nathaniel, the Dane who taught English at the local grade school. They say it with his British accent, which added even more flavor and fun to the moment.

When we got to Ongen's house, her husband met us. He made jokes and entertained us, reminding me of a jock or a ladies' man. Eventually,

Esther said we were going to head home, and at that Ongen's husband asked us to wait for a minute, and disappeared into his house for quite a long time.

I didn't understand why we were waiting, so after a while, I asked, "Esther, should we go?"

She knowingly said, "No, wait just a bit longer."

Soon Ongen's husband came out of his house and said he would walk us out. When we got to the end of his path, he gave each of us a hundred franc coin (worth about twenty cents) and told us to buy ourselves some tea. So generous! I felt like we were back in the 1920s and my grandpa had just given me spending money! We all calmly accepted his gift with two palms up and thanked him a lot.

As soon as we got far enough down the road to be out of earshot, Esther and Merci both held their coins up and broke into excited laughter. "We have money!" Their excitement was totally contagious, and I caught it in a flash, so we all started jumping and running down the road and waving our little coins. I've never been so excited about twenty cents! When we got back home, we rubbed Dinga's loss in her face, teasing her that because she was lazy and didn't walk Ongen home with us, she was a hundred francs poorer.

hard

A sadness has built up in my mind that I can't dissect. I can't pinpoint exactly where it's coming from, but it has left me struggling. I can feel the weight of the eighteen-hour-long night shift that has just come to an end, and as I walked home, every step felt heavy—I was "heavy stepped" and even heavier hearted. As I walked in the main entrance to our huts, Esther somehow understood with one glance. She came and grabbed my shoulders and asked me if I was hungry. I wasn't really, so she thought for a second and then said, "Come with me."

As we headed out, some of the boys started coming with us. Both Esther and I turned around at the same time, threw our hands up, and said in French, "GIRLS ONLY!" Then we looked at each other and laughed because our minds were so obviously on the same track.

We walked aimlessly along the weedy trails and she let me vent a bit. She listened while I pieced together big and complex thoughts using choppy elementary French.

Soon, we happened to arrive at her friend's house. Her friend, also maybe sixteen, was stirring supper, a mushy sauce and a boiling pot of rice. She wiped her hands on her wrap and greeted us with warm handshakes. Then she got us a bench and brought us water and bread.

I knew the little kids of this house because they hang out on the road where I ride horses. One of them is this super-stringy, big-mouthed, feisty girl named Lucie. While I was sipping my water, she started running her little fists in circles and saying in Nangjere, "Fight me, Emily. Come on, fight me!" She'd crouch down and scratch out the boundary of a boxing circle and then she would tap her hand on the ground all threatening like and circle her fists in the air and say again, "Come on, fight me!" I told her I didn't want to make her cry. I told her she was small, like a mosquito, and that I wasn't afraid. If anything could have made me feel that tomorrow was going to be a good day, it was the way this little rough-and-tough girl had it in her to fight me. Something about her spice reminded me that there's some fight left in me.

I really love the people here, but sometimes the work is really hard because I'm not fully trained and I frequently have to solve problems on my own in an unfamiliar language. That, combined with the sadness that comes from seeing people suffer, can really take you down. Wear you down. Put holes in you.

I'm trying to figure out how you get the downs to not bring you all the way down. How do you stay sensitive to the value of life and yet not become someone who's constantly mourning because of the people you see die? How do you encourage parents to take responsibility for their children's health and yet not become hard-hearted toward people who need a break, people who need financial help? How can you be content in a place like this?

As I wrote that last sentence, I looked at it and thought, *we AREN'T supposed to be content with a place like this! I AM supposed to look forward to a day when I won't see all this pain.* For now though, I need to find peace about it all. That would be nice.

naivety lets me go

Before I left home, there was a send-off meal for the children in the families with whom my brothers and I grew up. Many were going away to boarding schools or colleges, some of them in another country. After the meal was over, each of the parents spoke a few words of wisdom and release. My dad said a few things, but the one that has really stuck in my head is that in our youth and naivety, we don't know how hard certain things are and that is why we try them. This is what allows us to *do* things that people with more experience might not even attempt.

Once, back in high school, I got carried along by the hype of the moment and ate a big live beetle. Everyone in class was yelling, "Do it! Do it!" and offering money left and right. When the "bribe" reached forty-five dollars, I chomped down on that bug while its wings were still flapping. The taste was one of the bitterest I've ever known. I look back on that and wonder, *What were you thinking, Emily?* I think maybe for the right price I could do it again—though now, the right price would be huge! But it wasn't the money so much as it was my naivety and the challenge of the first time that pushed me to do it that day.

Last summer I was at Priest Lake with my family. Alex, Laura (my younger brother's girlfriend), and Nilmini (my older brother's fiancée) were there too. Late one day when Alex and I were sitting on the beach, we noticed a mountain across the lake and one of us said, "We should climb that. It's not THAT tall." Without any arguments or hesitation we jumped in a canoe, paddled across the lake, and started trekking up the mountain: no trail, no compass—just the goal of getting to the top.

The top of that mountain was a lot farther away than we had expected. On the hike, we got dirty, sweaty, and scraped up, but when we summited, we felt SO invincible! That's the naivety my dad was talking about—the way kids go for things without knowing what to expect or perhaps expecting only the best.

Yesterday, four other volunteers and I took a trip. We more or less "planned" it by tossing around a few ideas. We decided we would borrow bikes from our African friends and ride them to a village called Lai, about eighteen kilometers away on sandy roads.

We started riding around 8:30 A.M., carrying water, harmonicas, and bananas with us—all the essentials. The sand just grabs your tire and sucks it down, making the riding difficult. We hadn't gone more than two kilometers when we had our first bike accident, a minor one. Soon, bike wrecks were happening frequently, but they couldn't dampen the elation we were feeling. The music from our harmonicas gave an almost fairy-tale feel to the day—a feeling I hadn't had in a long, long while.

Part Six: Horse Riding

We reached Lai in just over two and a half hours. We probably could have made the trip in a much shorter time, but you have to understand that our bikes were ancient. One of my tires was doing some kind of tilting orbital rotation around the axle; I thought it would fall off at any moment. Ansley literally had bruises on her butt from sitting on a metal seat that had no padding, and Kristen could hardly control the direction her bike took in the sand.

The road ended at a wide, brown, slow-moving river, with Lai in sight on the other side. When we started this trip, we didn't know that the bridge was under construction, with about a hundred yards of it not done yet.

Shirtless men in dugout canoes offered to take us and our bikes across the river for about fifty cents. As we piled in, we noticed that they had stitched the cracks in their dugouts with thick rope. Don't ask me how you sew wood—I spent a lot of the boat ride trying to figure it out myself.

Setting long poles against the river's bottom, the boatmen pushed the boats along at a diagonal angle upstream and across the river, and the water bailer had a full-time job, essential to getting us to the other side.

In Lai, we sat down in a shabby makeshift restaurant. I still don't know what I ate; it was so rubbery that I felt like my teeth were on a trampoline. It came in a thin sauce that was glimmering with oil and was accompanied by two breadsticks speckled with flour mites.

Back at the river, we changed into our swimming suits behind the bushes. At the edge of a cliff, we found a place where we could make running leaps into the mucky, muddy water—probably not the cleanest thing I've ever done, but definitely not the most boring thing either!

The ride home was glorious, the sun setting right on the dirt path in front of us. Twenty-four miles on rickety bikes. Thanks naivety!

Part Seven

To Choose or Not to Choose

Have you heard people say that our lives are made up of all the choices we've made? That we're the drivers of our own cars and that we choose when we'll turn the steering wheel, pump the brakes, and put the pedal to the metal. I've always kind of thought that way. But what about the people whose mothers never took them where they could learn to drive a stick shift on a steep hill—and then are given a junky car and told they have to drive it blindfolded through hilly downtown Seattle at rush hour. Some people draw short sticks. They're dealt bad hands. We don't get to choose what comes to us. I'm not usually a patriotic flag-waver, but I sure do recognize that as an American, the balance has been tipped in my favor.

I'm so thankful I wasn't born in Chad.

There, I said it.

It seems like I shouldn't be saying that—like it's an unspoken truth that, when I speak it, reveals me as someone who has realized her luck and doesn't want to give it up.

But Africa is teaching me that freedom isn't found in our ability to choose every turn and rest stop on our highway. God knows that we've had to take detours because the road we chose was covered with obstacles we couldn't get over. We've had to deal with things we never chose, never asked for. Maybe our freedom lies in our being able to choose to keep moving no matter has happened to us. So many people here in Chad are doing just that. They don't have much, but they're using what they have to move in some direction they've chosen—directions like being kind, being honest, and getting an education.

this is a party

The other night I went to a party. A Chadian-style party. When I think of parties, I think of a certain atmosphere—you know, a celebration in which the host and guests bring good things to share and they all try to connect with each other.

I was really curious about whether partyers here would create that same atmosphere—actually, whether they would even be able to have a party because I didn't know where all of us would sit (chairs are a bit of a luxury here), what we would eat (do they have foods besides rice?), what we would talk about (languages are such a barrier), and whether we would listen to music (a staticky radio maybe?). I just couldn't imagine a party in Chad.

People started arriving, and I could tell everyone was hungry. We had been told that we didn't have to eat beforehand, that there would be a lot of food. I saw little "tables" all set up with mismatched "china." They served savory "crepes" and offered the choice of two different sauces, one of them vegetarian (non-goat!). The second course was juice, and the third course was rice *boule* (with more sauce), and by the time we ate that, we were full.

The vegetarian sauce was leafy green, which I knew wasn't a good party food because everyone who ate it would have green particles in their teeth. I was right; I could tell that people were a little self-conscious when they talked and everyone was running their tongues over their teeth. But then the host gave us each a toothpick—they had thought of everything!

We left the party full and went to sundown worship at the church. It was the beginning of the Sabbath, a day intended to give us rest after the work of the past week and a celebration of God's presence with us. After worship, we agreed that the party wasn't over yet and that we would all go back to the hut for a bonfire (which is rare in Chad because wood is so scarce), for singing, and for a fourth course of food.

The fire was going when we arrived, and our worship continued in singing accompanied by guitar and African drums. During the moments of silence that interspersed the singing, we felt a contentment that was a form of praise as well.

So, the Chadian party certainly was celebratory. I couldn't believe how they had used what they had to move us all toward celebration. The extravagance was in their generosity, not in what they put on the dinner table. It reminded me so much of the woman who had so little and gave it all. Jesus said that's what brought such meaning to her giving. What a party it is when people give you their best! You just feel it.

oh little girl

Josephine wailed all night again. Her foot certainly must hurt her; after all, it's infected down to the bone. But the instability of her mind is just amplifying her pain and causing her much distress and lack of peace. She has a little vial of ketamine, which we give to her when we're changing her dressing, and another ampoule of diazepam for the nights when she screams, keeping everyone in the hospital awake. But last night, the ampoule was empty. It was 1 A.M., and the night already seemed long because of a urinary-surgery patient whose catheter kept getting blocked with clots, and the irrigating flow of water had to be watched or his bladder could swell and he would have awful pain.

I peeked around the corner to make sure Josephine wasn't trying to climb out of her bed in an attempt to go home, something she has done numerous times. What I saw was unfair. I saw both strength and weakness in a child all at once.

In the midst of all her crying, Josephine called her seven-year-old granddaughter, who was sleeping on the cement floor, until she finally sat up. The child was exhausted. Then Josephine said something in Nangjere that obviously meant, "Come up on the bed with me." The little girl followed orders, climbed up on the bed, and sat behind her grandmother. Then Josephine took the little girl's arms and wrapped them around herself while she continued crying. The little girl didn't know what to do for her grandmother, who was rocking back and forth and wailing. The girl's eyes were wide, and I could tell she was just plain scared.

Pulling Josephine's grip off the little girl, I set her bare little feet back down on the cement and said, "You can sleep." The sweet child quietly lay back down while Josephine latched onto my hand and cried some more.

I wanted to scold Josephine for waking up her granddaughter and scaring her, but I know that mental disease is so often no one's fault. It makes *me* want to cry.

I saw the strength of this little girl when I came to help her off the bed. She had tears in her eyes, but none of them were falling. She was so strong for her grandma.

Her weakness lay in the fact that she couldn't choose to be in any other situation. Every day she helps prepare the food for her grandma, she looks after her baby sister, and she brings her grandmother the water she needs to take her meds. I wish Josephine's leg would get better so the girl can leave this hospital. It's no place for her.

the man in the red underwear

I went to the river again this afternoon—just needed a break by myself. But today I wasn't by myself. There was a little old man with a long branch of a tree that he was using as a fishing pole. When he finished fishing, he stripped down to some very old red underwear, and then he sat on the bottom of the river, his ribbed torso sticking out above the surface of the water, and he splashed himself.

I began swimming against the current, letting it push against me, feeling good about this attempt at exercise. I breathed on my right side every other stroke, and I kept my eyes closed. But then I had this uneasy feeling. I stood up in the water and looked over to where my horse was tied up—or to where she HAD BEEN tied up. GONE!

Looking all around, I caught sight of her cantering off into the brush. In my very American swimsuit—which no African would wear; they don't wear things like that—I ran up the bank and after the horse. When finally I caught her, I walked back to the river, back to the man in the red underwear. He told me I had good luck and that I should *"bien attaché"* the *"cheval"* next time.

I was embarrassed. But then I remembered that when you're embarrassed, imagining the people around you in their underwear is supposed to make you feel better. I didn't even have to use my imagination! Ha!

bedsprings

Esther was lying on our old set of bedsprings, which sits on a bare steel frame. We've jammed a collage of retired shirts, pants, and other material between the springs to act as padding. I told Esther to make room for me, and she moved over till she took only half of the bed. Then she asked me if I was going to sleep outside. I said, "Yeah, right here with you." So she got a blanket, and we tucked ourselves in. Our bodies were close because the bed was stubbornly narrow.

Sleeping with Esther reminded me of sleeping with my cousins Mindy and Lisa, missionary kids who used to come to our home and live with us while they were on furlough from Africa. Lisa is a heater and a sprawler. Despite the unspoken three-way division of the bed, Lisa's body has always taken whatever space it wanted to.

Jolie and Esther prepare the sauce for the evening meal.

Draped across me. Pushing close to Mindy.
Her legs sliding into my space.
Moving and fidgeting as they wished.

In the middle of the night, I woke up with Esther's head on my shoulder, her arm linked through mine, one leg flopped over my trapped body, and breathing right into my eyes. I felt like we were blood sisters.

When I awoke in the morning, Esther was already sweeping the courtyard. I sat up with groggy eyes and said a long sleepy, *"Laaaaaapppppppp-pia."* As I stood up, Esther laughed at the way the metal bedsprings had imprinted patterns on my legs and shoulder, and we decided we need to add more scrap clothes to the padding on the springs.

poor

I pulled on my Nike runners and changed into my university service day T-shirt and the tasseled Indian pants that I sewed myself. (The tassels swing around my ankles and tickle them as I walk.) Then I waited until Izeedoor got up. He doesn't have an alarm clock, so I can't blame him for being a few minutes late. He's sleepy eyed and rubs his hands together and moves extremely slowly when he wakes up. Our neighbor Tabgue, who is eighteen and likes to ask me about the "truths of America," came too. We're doing a 5 A.M. run.

We started out, but after just a few strides, Izeedoor suddenly stopped. I turned around, intending to tell him to pick it up, but then I realized what he needed to do. I laughed and said I would keep running while he took care of business right there on the side of the road. He caught up with us in a minute or two, and we wound through the village and out into the country. I was surprised at how many people we passed at that hour, heading to the rice fields with sharp rice blades and water containers balanced on their heads as they walked. As we passed them and greeted them with nods, they turned around slowly, keeping their buckets steady but intrigued by the speed with which we moved at this hour in the morning.

The sun began to rise, and it was a jaw-dropping sunrise! I thought, *Maybe this is magic; the magic of God.* It was a miracle of beauty! Seriously, my heart jumped at least four times. I can't stop talking about something that pretty. The sun cast itself up onto clouds and threw shots of different colors all about. All of this light came from one big round ball of fire that was rising quicker than it does anywhere else I've been. I couldn't help but run backwards so I could watch it come. Our pace was perfect, and our breathing was so synchronized. We ran a solid 5k and returned home to shower out of our buckets and eat something mushy and warm.

I don't see poverty much anymore. I used to see it all the time. The dirty-handed little kids. Awful, old rusted bikes. Clothing tinted brown from dirt. Noses dripping with snot. No one wearing shoes. Kids playing with bottle caps and dirty plastic bags and eating plain, dirt-covered potatoes. Pants so outgrown that the wearers can't zip them up anymore. Dirt houses. Holes for toilets. Leaves for toilet paper. You know, poverty.

But now I've lived in a dirt house, played with bottle caps, gone barefoot, and found my clothes wearing thin with holes in random places, and the kinds of poverty that I used to think needed to be solved right away aren't what I now consider to be the most pressing hardships of this place. I see the deeper poverty in the sadness of the mother who lost her fifteen-year-old to a fast-moving case of meningitis and in Poly's mother, who lay in his bed while he bled internally for so long and then died about a week ago. It's the poverty of the malnourished children. These kinds of suffering make me angry and frustrated. Having less isn't such a bad thing, but losing hope as many people who suffer do—that's so hard for me to watch. But the most difficult thing for me to realize and admit is that we have even bigger losses of hope in the States.

the right thing might be wrong?

A young Arab girl lies limp across her father's arms. Her colorful necklace mimics her body and falls limp on her neck and shoulder. Her hemoglobin has fallen to a level of two, very low. She needs blood.

They check her blood type. She is A positive.

Then each of her family members is also checked. The policy here is that we check the family first. If they have matching blood, then it is their responsibility to give it for their daughter. When none of the family members are matching donors, then volunteers and hospital staff can give blood.

In this case, the girl's father was a perfect match. They told him that he should go to the lab and give blood for her right away or she would die.

At first he didn't respond. Then he said something in Arabic.

The bed, with padded rags, that Esther and I shared for a night.

A local translated his words. "I don't want to give" is what he had said.

WHAT! At first I thought that maybe I had heard wrong, or that he had misunderstood the gravity of the situation. The severity of the girl's condition was explained again. And again, his answer was No, he wouldn't give. He didn't want to give his blood for his daughter.

He was pressed for the reason. Was it fear? Some

religious belief? He gave no reason.

It made me so angry. I don't know Arabic, but I couldn't help myself—I marched over to where he was sitting next to his curled-up daughter and gave him a piece of my mind in a mix of English and French. It's amazing what hand signals and facial expressions can do. He just sat there and stared off into the distance. (OK, so I guess they don't do that much.) The family was sent away—told that if they weren't willing to fight for their daughter's health, the hospital couldn't do anything.

I went to Augustan, who had sent the family away, and I said, "Augustan, I am A positive too. Let me give."

He said, "No. This is the family's responsibility. If people learn that they can be irresponsible and someone else will pick up their responsibility for their child, everyone will do this."

I REALLY respect Augustan, but at the same time I couldn't justify that little girl's dying a preventable death to teach a lesson. It wasn't her fault that her father wouldn't give blood.

That was a really unsettling night. There has to be a better system. That's easy to say, but I have no idea what would work better. Systems, systems, systems. I know they're necessary, but I sure am not a fan of the ones I've seen lately.

What if something that's the wrong thing to do in one situation is the right thing to do in another? I so often wonder if we don't underestimate God's unpredictability. He did bring His Son into the world through an unwed mother, and His Son ate with the tax collectors. And when the system required the stoning of the adulteress, He offered forgiveness.

I'm having a hard time knowing what the right thing is. Is the system wrong sometimes? Is the right thing wrong sometimes? Bah.

tandem biking

Three weeks left. It's not every day that I'm in Africa. Yes, right now it seems to me that I *am* in Africa every day since I've been here for five months. But despite that feeling, the truth is that this day in Africa is a very exceptional day compared to the rest of my life. So, I've been trying to make as many memories, experience as many things, and learn as many lessons as I can in this last stretch. There is a motto that I've tried to adopt.

It goes, "If you are given a moment and you could either let it pass you by or make a memory, always make the memory!"

So the other day, I took my camera and went on a long walk in search of things to photograph. I knew my mom would have had a fit if she knew how few pictures I'd actually taken up to this point.

As I walked out of town and toward the river, a wrinkly, elderly man came riding up beside me on one of those rickety bikes that I've written about. *"Lapia, Lapia, Lapia! LAPIA BUJA!"*

OK, little guy, calm down, I thought.

He stopped his bike to talk, and when he found out that we were going in the same direction, he told me that I could ride on the back of his bike.

Wow! Like hitchhiking! I would never in my life pass up a chance like that. So, I sat on the little metal rack behind the bike seat and hung my legs down in case the takeoff wasn't as smooth as we wished. He tried to get going, but I was definitely bigger than he was. His frail little leg muscles just couldn't push us down the sandy path on this dying bicycle. So we decided that I would give it a go and he would ride on the back.

That worked a lot better.

The bike got tipsy in a few places, and there were times when I thought for sure we were going to take a tumble. However, we pulled it off. I even managed to take a snapshot of the two of us while riding the bike.

We rode a few miles—this was no short jaunt—and I asked him a couple of times, "Should we turn here? Should we stop here?" He always hurriedly shrieked his answer: "No! Not yet! I'll tell you. I'll give you warning before the road comes!" I think he was worried that if we stopped, we wouldn't get going again.

Eventually, we got to the next village, and the little man introduced me to his family and one of his wives, and then they started making plans to feed me. I knew that it was getting dark, and I still had to run back three miles. The sun had already set when I finally started jogging. It got darker and darker, and I started passing some interesting types of people. One straggly looking man was walking in snake patterns, and his eyes hardly focused. Rice wine had gotten him good. I picked up my pace and sent cautious glances over my shoulder from time to time. Soon, a young boy came up beside me on his bike and started talking to me with all of the English he knew. "Hello how are you I am fine where are you going what is your name?" he said in one long stream. He sure knew how to get the conversation going. He accompanied me all the way home. Not that I'm afraid of the dark or anything.

sexually active

I told my parents about Dinga's heart some time back. I could tell they really cared. Then a few days ago, my dad, who is a family practice doctor in Spokane, Washington, wrote me this e-mail.

> Emily, we know your days are full now. I have thought of Dinga often since you first told us of her—what a tough situation. Most foreign help would need some basic info. She must see a cardiologist and have an echocardiogram at minimum or no one will know where to start. Can Dr. James arrange it with Samedi's help? What about the brother of Samedi in N'Djamena—the one with government influence? You could leave some money to help get that started. Mom has already checked with Loma Linda University Heart International as to how they work, and we will continue to look at a couple other organizations. In the meantime she needs to get a basic evaluation. I would not hold out unrealistic hope, but those steps at least would also sort out whether medications may help as well. Sometimes beta-blockers are a big help, and they are very cheap.
>
> See what you can do, and we will, too, and we will all pray.

It's not easy to *not* have unrealistic hope—not when it's about someone you love. But Dad is right; these first steps are ones we can take. I talked to Samedi over supper last night, and he said he could arrange for Dinga to get an ID card, which she'll need in order to travel to Cameroon, where an echocardiogram can be done. Gary and Wendy (the mission pilot and his wife) offered to let her fly with them on one of their trips over to Cameroon once she has all the necessary paperwork.

When I talked to my dad yesterday, he voiced another concern—that if Dinga got pregnant, her heart might not hold up under the pressure. He said I needed to make sure she wasn't sexually active—that she understood it was a risk that could take her life.

I didn't know how I was going to bring this topic up. I don't know if the topic is taboo, and I don't know if it is something that would even affect Dinga—she is fourteen, after all. And then there's my French, which is decent now, but not really adequate for a conversation that needs to be tactful and well articulated.

I take three-year-old Armelle to the river for the first time in her life.

Today, as Esther, Dinga, and I were sifting rice, I said, "So, do young girls—your age—sleep with boys often?" Both of them snickered and smiled. I smiled back but played stupid, asking, "What? What's funny?"

Esther, who is a bit older than Dinga, tackled my question. "Yes," she said. "Sometimes."

Then, when Dinga wasn't looking, Esther pointed to her. Dinga caught her out of the corner of her eye, swatted at her shoulder, and began to laugh, and she denied what Esther was implying. Esther went a step further, saying that Dinga had many boyfriends.

The conversation wound along funny pathways for a while but eventually became more serious. I asked whether they were ready to have children. Both of them said, "No!" Then I told Dinga that people were trying to get help for her heart but that if she were to become pregnant, her heart might not last long enough to be fixed. Esther was translating this complicated message into the local dialect for Dinga, and when she stopped talking, I asked her, "Does Dinga understand?" Dinga herself said, "Yes," and I could tell she did.

baby, let me sing to you

I got home late and ran into Jolie, who was just leaving to go see her sister. I said, "I'm just a bit hungry, Jolie. Is there any food left?" She said that they had saved me some and that Cecil would bring it to me. I sat down in the pitch-black night outside Cecil's house, and soon she brought out a small wicker basket that held several glowing coals. She handed me a tin plate that held a round ball of rice and peanut sauce on the side.

For some reason, all the children were gone, and the surrounding huts were silent—all the children except sweet baby Galas.

Cecil was pregnant when I came to Chad in September. She was incredibly shy, and at first I thought she didn't like me much. She would often tell me with a serious look on her face that my clothes weren't good or that I didn't know how to cook. One time she even told me I was dirty and needed to bathe! A brief smirk always followed her insults and then she'd escape to another part of the house before I figured out how to respond. I just didn't understand her. After a while, though, I noticed that she was doing sweet things for me, like bringing me snacks and teaching me how to shake rice. So, our friendship grew.

I kept asking Cecil when the baby would come. I told her I wanted to go to the hospital with her when she was going into labor and that she should knock on my hut door if it was during the night. Then, when I woke up one morning, all the children said Cecil's baby had been born in the night. I ran to her hut and asked, "Why didn't you come get me?" She exclaimed, "Emily, you sleep so much! I tried to call for you through your window, but you told me you were sleeping and tired." I apologized over and over, telling her that I didn't remember saying that at all. I hate talking in my sleep. It gets me in trouble all the time. This time I had missed the birth of a baby brother. *Grrr.* But Cecil let me hold Galas, and I gave her the bouquet of balloons I had made for her.

Cecil kept Galas indoors for the first six weeks or so—rarely leaving the hut. But now he was big, with cute baby fat. And on this night it was baby Galas who cried in the quiet night. I finished eating while Cecil was tending to things around her hut, so I picked Galas up and tried to rock him to sleep. But he was hungry and just kept crying. So then I started singing. I sang whatever came to me, rambling off my own made-up lullabies. Anyone who heard me singing could only imagine how clever—or not!—the lyrics were. No one in Béré could understand my English, and no one in America will ever hear those songs. Africa is a safe place to be yourself!

I stopped singing when I realized Galas had been asleep for some time. Then I asked myself, *Do you realize what you're doing, Emily? You're singing lullabies to an African baby outside his hut by the light of a coal fire!* These are the moments I'm living for here. I have to notice them and remember them, because there are other moments when all I want is to be transported home.

Part Eight

My Dilemma

I've taken on a new life here, something from the past. I wash my clothes by hand now. I walk everywhere. I shower from a bucket and sleep on a grass mat.

And while these things made me do a whole lot of adjusting in the beginning, sometimes now I wonder what it will be like to do it any differently.

The seventeen kids.

Jolie's Arabic perfume.

Aaron's constantly open fly.

The never-ending jabber.

Rice and enormous amounts of oil.

Mounden saying he's hungry still after all the food is gone.

The rusted metal bedsprings that we love to lie on.

Last night, I sat cross-legged in the dark, possessed by a very quiet, watchful kind of mood. I watched everyone accused Dinga of stealing Jolie's silky nightgown—the one she wears for Samedi only. Dinga's buttons were pushed, and she blushed brightly and shouted a jumbled defense. Then Jolie made Aaron cry by telling him he couldn't sit next to her because his legs were "white with dirt." Esther began singing "Head and Shoulders, Knees and Toes" in English but kept getting her anatomy all wrong. Jolie told me that Alex had called her that day and told her that he didn't like me anymore and that I shouldn't come back to America. *"Urra Americ di, Emily"* (Don't go to America, Emily). Tony piped up very seriously that Jolie was a liar and that Alex *didn't* call her. Tony's so honest! I told him I'd be in tears if it weren't for him. I could tell he felt proud of his honesty.

As time rolled along and we moved deeper into the night hours, the kids quieted down and the mats held a pile of bodies—much like pick-up sticks, sprawled out and crossing one another and all of them in their sleep tugging at the covers they shared.

Goma, the irresistible two-year-old grandchild who lay curled up at the foot of my chair, started crying after Pabris pulled all the covers off of him. I reached one hand down to him, and he reached two up to me. I pulled him up to my lap, and in five seconds, he was asleep again.

It was nearly ten thirty, and Jolie said it was time to get all the kids into the hut to sleep. They HATE being moved after they've fallen asleep—just as American kids do. But they'll get eaten by the mosquitoes if they don't go in, so Esther comes around shaking all of them and telling them to go inside. When they don't move, she lifts their arms and pulls their upper bodies off the floor and then lets them go, and they drop floppily to the ground, and there's LOTS of whining and crying—*sooooo* much whining. I picked Aaron up and hauled his dead weight in, laid him on the mat, and then went back for Armelle.

What will I do when I have to leave them? Can you see my dilemma?

At times I'm stressed and homesick beyond belief and want nothing more than to be far, far away from here, and at other times, I can't imagine the day I get on the plane. These are the delicate balances that tip from side to side. I've been split, and now I'm aware that I have more than one very good thing.

tb: tired but

Have you ever walked into a church that was empty? I'm sure you have. There's that silence that's somehow a sound of its own. Imagine that sound, but instead of carpet and hymnals, picture metal beds and spiders' webs. It's OK for you to picture a pulpit because there actually still is one in this place, all lonely in the front. Then imagine that your breathing is a little shallow because you keep thinking about all the tuberculosis that lives in the sanctuary. Breathing deeply seems risky, so your subconscious keeps you from doing it.

Despite the ghetto environment, this place has a mystical, recuperative atmosphere that is linked to the community of those who are all living under the same roof in what seems to be one big, drafty dorm room. Tall, skinny church windows climb the walls every five feet and about twenty metal beds (some with and some without mattresses) randomly occupy the floor.

The old church is being used as the tuberculosis ward.

The people who are diagnosed at the hospital are given free treatment through a program called DOT: Directly Observed Treatment. This means that someone watches them take their pills each morning to ensure that they get better, because if you don't treat TB *consistently* for a full three months, it won't ever go away. So these people have this experience—which we hope is a once-in-a-lifetime thing—of living together under the church roof while ridding their bodies of TB.

I used some of the money that one of my good friends sent to buy paint; now, the next two weeks will be a painting marathon. We'll be painting big murals with whatever colors we can mix and make. The hospital is turning what is now the TB ward into a pediatrics ward, and the TB patients will move into some newly constructed mud-brick rooms—perhaps two to a room instead of this communal living style. With these changes, we'll do a better job of confining the germs, and the new pediatrics ward will be triple the size of the current one, allowing us to care for many more babies.

When I walked into the TB ward this afternoon, it was almost empty. The only person still there—a man—was sitting in his bed. He was attached to an IV (he probably was being treated for malaria on top of TB) and couldn't go outside into the sun like the rest of the patients tend to do during the day. He just sat with his legs hanging down off the edge of the bed. I had to do a double take because I couldn't tell whether there were legs in his pants, he was just so skinny. The rapid loss of weight is one of the symptoms of TB.

I said, *"Lapiaga?"* which means something like, "How well is it going?"

He s-l-o-w-l-y reached up, took my hand, and said almost in a whisper, *"Lapia,"* which means something like, "Well."

Then he turned the question around, asking me, *"Lapiaga?"*

I said, *"On gillia di di"* (I'm a little tired).

Without missing a beat, in that same whisper, he said, *"Kouma ma bumma"* (God will give it).

I agreed, but then thought about his situation and wondered what God has given him. But he hadn't told me what God would give, just that He would give it.

I think I'm going to paint that on the walls somewhere: "God will give it." Then people will ask, "What is 'it'?" and no one will have the answer because our hope rests in the fact that God is big and complex and beyond us and that's what we want Him to be, isn't it?

Will He give me rest?

Maybe not.

Health?

Maybe not.

Sickness may continue, but hope will also continue—and loss of hope seems much heavier to bear than sickness is. I'm tired, BUT *kouma ma bumma.*

cleaning is messy

This morning, I asked Augustan to help me hire some of the TB patients to clean the entire TB ward. He came, and we hired four men. We didn't give them a wage right then, but we assured them that we would give them a little something if they helped. So the five of us moved all of the beds out of the ward and placed them under the mango trees in the courtyard. Then we scrubbed all of the walls with brooms and soap. One of the guys was throwing soapy water up on the walls, three of us scrubbed with brooms, and another rinsed with a hose. The water ran brown off the walls, and soon we were standing in these warm lakes. Then we started using the already dirty water, to loosen who-knows-what off the remaining walls. For a while, they let me have the job of throwing the soapy water up on the wall, but I was terrible at it—the soaped-up bowl kept slipping out of my hand, and I was getting everyone wet. You may be thinking I'm just uncoordinated, but it's harder to throw water up a wall than you think! One time, I totally missed the wall and the water went all over the men. Good thing they know how to laugh—but even so, they took the job away from me at that point.

After a while, I filled two jars with water and then added some drink mixes that Jacob, a volunteer from Chicago, left behind. The mixes are called Greens To Go. They have lots of flaky green pieces that look like lettuce or spinach. They resemble what I imagine the ocean would look like if you took eggbeaters to the kelp. The drinks are completely unappetizing to the eyes, but they have lots of vitamins in them, and using this argument, I got all of the workers to drink the stuff—skeptical though they were. They were happy for a break because we had been working hard.

After we had scrubbed everything, even the high ceiling, we shoveled the water out of the sanctuary—which felt like shoveling snow off of sidewalks. When we finished, the room was beautiful—"proper" as they liked to call it. Then the men asked if they could pour the leftover bleach down the rat holes. They hate rats. I've never seen their faces so expressive as when they were telling me about the rats coming in the middle of the night and running around their beds and across their chests. Sarah suggested we buy a cat to live in the sanctuary. Anyway, it was absolutely clean, and while I wouldn't have licked the floor, I probably would have slept on it—which is saying a lot.

I was impressed by how hard the men worked. They didn't stop once, and they would have taken my work from me rather than stop working. When it was time for me to pay, I went back to Augustan and told him that the men had worked really hard and I wanted to pay them well. I asked him how much I should pay them. He said two dollars—they will think that's a lot. Two dollars—it's double a day's wage here. So I gave them each a thousand francs, and they accepted their money with two hands—a sign of gratitude. I love the gesture. After I had paid them, they asked, "Emily, can we have the leftover soapy water to wash our clothes?" Yes. Yes. You most definitely can. So all the wives came and filled their buckets. They'll be all proper for tomorrow when we start the painting.

I still haven't taken a shower. I need to badly—I feel like I must have TB germs in my ears and nose and eyes and mouth! But today was *so* satisfying. This change of pace and purpose is everything my heart needed.

guts

Dr. Ted Howe, Ansley's dad, came to Chad for a visit. Tonight, Ansley's African family cooked Ansley, Ted, and me a dinner in honor of his visit. In fact, they killed their goat—which is a big deal. I was very interested in how the goat was prepared. I watched as the mother pulled and cut, pulled and cut at the tissues and organs. When she pulled out the intestines, they hung like snakes across her hands. She cut them open and then used her thumb and forefinger to squeeze into the fire the remnants of what the goat had eaten in his last days, leaving the intestines empty. She dropped the intestines into a bucket of water and washed them like a vegetable, and then set them over the fire, where they cooked.

It was dark when Ansley's African family was finally ready to serve the meal. Ansley, Ted, and I sat on a mat, feeling incredibly honored. The special meal was like a big present that they were giving us. It's a moment I won't forget. Then they placed a big bowl in the middle of our little triangle; it contained all the guts of the goat—all of its innards, the most delicate pieces of meat.

Ansley, Ted, and I spoke in English among ourselves, using very pleasant tones and high pitches so as not to give away the fact that we were discussing the strength of our stomachs—whether we'd be able to make it through the meal. But we felt a surge of courage, and we mentally relabeled the food in front of us. We weren't eating to nourish our bodies. This meal was an opportunity to nourish the relationships that we valued so much.

So, Ted decided that we would each reach into the dark bucket and pull out pieces of organs, which we would then give to each other—and we had to eat what we were given. Ansley pulled out a hunk of liver and handed it to Ted. He pulled out a portion of the heart and handed it to me. And I pulled out a bit of the intestines and gave it to Ansley.

I can actually say that much of the meat was all right, although some pieces tasted like a farm. But it was goat meat, so that makes sense.

let her cry

Her baby is dying, and she's the only one who cares at this point—and you want her to quit with the tears? Let them flow, I say; I'm glad that SOMEONE'S heart is hurting for this baby.

Dr. Ted, Ansley's dad, is here visiting. He, Ansley, and I all went to the market earlier in the day. As we were walking the dirt path home, a woman passed us, her pace brisk and hurried. She had her baby stiffly propped up and over her shoulder, and as she passed we could see that the baby's eyes were rolled back into his head and his little mouth foamed with saliva. His seizing made Dr. Ted's heart break—I could tell by the way his voice got softer and his brow tensed up. I felt hopeless for that baby and also anxious about the night shift I was going to work. The baby we were following back to the hospital might die under my watch.

When I got to work that afternoon, sure enough, there he was—a sweet, small baby with big legs, lying on the bare mattress of bed 4. His mom lay with him, staring silently and fixedly at his pulsing chest.

Dr. Francois was on duty. He decided to do a lumbar puncture to test the baby for meningitis. The test cost three dollars. That meant putting together the puzzle of finding the money. You get your friend to give you twenty-five cents. You trade in a medicine that you bought recently, and you give the hospital your phone to hold as security until you can find the rest of the money you need somewhere.

The baby's mom couldn't watch the doctor perform the lumbar puncture, so I took over, clasping the baby's legs and neck and bending his body into a compact C-shape while the doctor did the puncture. The spinal fluid came out, but instead of being clear, it was a murky gray—a sure sign of meningitis. This diagnosis will start more searching for money because the test to determine what disease you have is only the first process that will be needed to bring recovery.

When the results were confirmed, we came back to give them to the mother and to discuss the treatment plan. As my headlamp dimly lit up her face, I saw quiet rivers running down her cheeks. She avoided my sympathetic gaze, but Dr. Francois laid into her immediately. "Stop this crying!" he commanded, his finger pointed at the tears streaming down her face. "What is this? You think this crying is going to do something for your baby? Give your baby milk," he tapped at the mother's breasts, "and put sugar on his tongue. And QUIT CRYING!"

The mother looked panicked and, understanding his crude gesture, tried to nurse the baby. But she hadn't understood the rest of his fast French explanation—she spoke only the local dialect.

As we turned and walked to the next bed, I couldn't bite my tongue any longer. "Why can't she cry? Because you don't like crying? She doesn't know what to do for her baby. She has no idea!" I was so upset that I had to leave, so I went to the desk in the other room and did some paperwork.

Dr. Francois is fresh out of medical school. He's here for just one year. When he first arrived, everyone was impressed with his dedication to and compassion for the patients, but this place has rubbed him a little raw too.

115

A few minutes later, he spoke to me in accented English. "Emily, I don't want you to have a bad impression of me," he began.

I said, "No, it's not that. It's just that Africa is so different." I was thankful he had started in English because I really wanted to communicate a certain message without scrambling for the right words.

I continued, "When I look at that lady, I just think, *Africa is hard! Her baby has a horrible disease that is wreaking havoc on his little body. Let her cry!* Why is it that in Africa you have to be so tough and you aren't allowed to feel these things as they are? I mean, did you see how the woman jumped to do every little thing you asked her to do for her baby? She went and bought sugar, she fed him, they searched high and low for money. She hasn't been to school. She doesn't know anything about fevers, about convulsions, about hypoglycemia. She's helpless to do anything, and convulsions are scary. Let her cry."

Dr. Francois explained that he is tired of people doing little for the health of their children, which I could understand. He also said that he hadn't thought about her not knowing what would help her child or understanding the language he was using. I think we understood each other. We've got to talk about these things because we learn from each other.

The rest of the night was hard. Two babies cried almost all night long. I can't rest because I feel like there's something I have to be doing when really, it's all been done. After all the perfusions have been hung, after all the wet cloths have been laid on the feverish bodies and they've been given acetaminophen, after all the Valium has been administered to stop the seizing, everything is just left to—honestly, sometimes I feel like it is left to some kind of lottery in which some children will get better and some will lose their lives.

At 2 A.M. I lie down to rest next to Kristen. We're lying on the emergency room floor, which has seen more blood than I care to think about. And even though we have a blanket to pad our heads, the cement and the situation and the fact that malaria is winning in the room next to me—makes everything feel hard.

I've never felt so anxious—as though no solution is the only solution. I feel as though if I don't stay on my toes, death will come right under my heels, and it's unthinkable. So every ten minutes I find myself at the bedside of the babies who are the worst off—just looking at them. Why am I doing this? The babies that will die despite treatment will die. There's nothing more to do—nothing but go to their bedsides and touch their stomachs and look to see if they're breathing.

God, give us *peace* for the things that we aren't big enough, smart enough, or powerful enough to control. But keep us fleshy too—fleshy and caring and doing whatever we can.

pots

For our worship on Friday nights, we've been listening to *The Pineapple Story*. It's a story told by a funny man about his mission experience in New Guinea. His goal was to start a garden to help the people—to give them fresh fruits. But the situation became problematic when the people kept stealing all of the pineapples out of his garden—the very garden that he was starting to help them! He tried all sorts of things to keep them from stealing, none of which worked. Finally, out of deep frustration, he surrendered his efforts. He told God, "You know what? I'm trying to do this for You anyway. These are Your pineapples, God. If You don't want them stolen, then do something." Then the man started spreading the word that he had given his pineapple field to God—that it was no longer his. Soon after, everyone stopped stealing pineapples, because they couldn't justify stealing from God.

I love this idea—the complete surrender of the things you have. Some great sense of peace comes with the realization that we really have only our bodies, our thoughts, and our actions—people can take everything else away from us while we're on this earth. I feel like I would worry less about things and become more generous with that type of surrender.

I've been painting murals inside the TB ward for four days now, and things are starting to shape up. The other workers—the TB patients—who'd had no painting experience before, have learned a lot. I gave them rollers and asked them to paint a base coat of blue on all the walls. The plan was that I would paint the murals on top of this base coat.

However, when the first batch of blue ran out, my painters started mid wall with a whole different shade. I ran over and said, "Use the same color! This is different; I can see a line where you switched blues." They responded by saying, "It's the same color, Emily—blue and blue!" I think they just don't see the line of contrast between the two shades. So, we're taking the mishaps and mess-ups in stride. When it's finished, we'll call it abstract, deep, and meaningful, so we can say that anyone who questions

our techniques just doesn't have the artful eye that these Chadian painters did.

Since this TB ward will be turned into the new pediatrics ward in a
few months, I've been redecorating it: Painting big, branchy trees and
winding rivers full of fish. Adding colorful bubbles and checkerboard
print. Making huge sunbeams light up flocks of birds. And I've written,
"God will give it" on the wall near the entrance. Yesterday, I brought
Mounden, Crispen, and Pabris here, traced their bodies on a wall, and
filled the tracings in with white. You can definitely tell who each tracing
represents; as the boys grow, they'll be able to come back and see how
they've changed.

Every day, people come, requesting "just a little bit" of paint. The first
day it was John Jac, the gate guard and night watchman. He wanted a little
paint in a cup so he could paint the bed in his "watchtower." Then there
was Degal, the other night watchman and maintenance man. He wanted
me to paint his family name plate—a rusted rectangular metal sheet nailed
to his mud-hut wall—a bright color and then write his name—all three
names—along with his title at the hospital. I painted it bright orange. I'm
not sure it's what he had in mind because when I gave it to him he didn't
say much except "Orange!"

Then there are the women. They come every day with their metal pots.
The original factory paint coat has chipped away in some places, and bits of
silver-colored metal show through. It doesn't look bad. In fact, I've seen my
mom come home with things like that from antique stores. But they have
this idea in their heads that it's better to have paint on all parts of the pot. So,
they come and dip their fingers in different colors and smear red, green, and
yellow into the chipped places. Now the pots look real . . . unique. I can't
help but laugh. Such little things seem to make them very happy.

I did think for a second, *Oh man, Emily, if you start giving out paint,
EVERYONE will want paint.* But then I thought about the pineapple story.
My paint is nowhere close to running out; it isn't mine anyway, and if God
wants it splotched on pots around Béré, I'm all for it.

outdoors

I have five days left. That's a short enough time to make me realize what
a good thing I have here in Africa. It's a short enough time that all nega-

tives evaporate in the warmth of the love I feel. It's too bad that we have to be looking at an end to really value what was there since the beginning. These last few weeks we've been sleeping outside every night. It's blazing hot during the days now. I've noticed that Samedi and Jolie have been resting at home in the evenings. Whether or not they're doing it on purpose, it has certainly given us some priceless times together just before I leave. I come around the corner and see that everyone is out on the mats. I lie down, and Jolie starts rambling in dialect, sending orders all around, and despite the speed at which she speaks and the complicated grammar she uses, I'm able to gather from her words and tone and motions that she ordered someone to get me tea, someone to bring me a pillow, and someone else to spread out her blanket for me to lie on. She's the sweetest!—the kind of sweet that leaves you feeling completely undeserving.

The kids aren't supposed to be on her blanket because they haven't bathed, but the rules always fade and soon the kids are all in a line on either side of me. I pull my own sheet over me and toss my blue fleece blanket over both Dinga and myself. Armelle is to my right and completely naked. I try to throw the other edge of the blanket over her, but she throws it off because she's hot. There's some jabbering and singing, some crying and fighting, and soon everyone is asleep. I wake up a couple of times—once to a dog licking my face, another time to Esther coming home from a party, and what woke me the third time makes me laugh even now.

It must have been two in the morning or so when *I woke to someone pulling off my covers!* I didn't move but instead, just opening my eyes, I watched as Tony pulled my sheet off of me hand over hand, leaving Dinga and me to share the little fleece. He sneaked back over to the far corner of the mat and lay down, wrapping my sheet all around him. I laughed hard but silently and decided that if he was willing to steal my covers, he must be miserably cold, and then I found my way back to sleep.

The next morning, the hazy light woke us up and everyone started guessing what time it was. Four thirty. Five. Six. Everyone was cold by this time, and those who weren't already in our little lineup squeezed in so we were like ten or so bundles all in a row. I narrowed my eyes and asked Tony if he was *nice and warm*. A huge smile broke out on his face as I told everyone about his thieving. I think he simultaneously loved and hated being caught.

Mounden said, "Let's go running—it's nice and cold!" I said, "Yeah!

Let's run!" and stood up, and then, realizing the depth of my fatigue, I fell back down onto Jolie's rock-hard pillow, saying, "Let's NOT run!" Mounden moaned and protested, but we lay there a long while, until Esther started sweeping the yard as she does every morning. Her sweeping sent dust all over us. And so the day began.

the way we sleep

Last night, Ansley came to sleep outside at my house with the kids and me. At about 9:30, Samedi came home from his night shift for a short visit. Coming around the corner and stopping at the sight of this ocean of bodies sprawled out, he said, "Ooo la la! All of these people are for Samedi?" I think the size of his family surprises even him sometimes. Anyway, we all chanted, "Yes! Yes! All of us!"

Tony and Mounden were feeling especially talkative, and we discussed all sorts of things, ranging from Mounden's future career to Tony's lack of money to the people whose characters they admired the most.

Ansley falls asleep so fast! The kids kept waking her up, saying, "Our professor is asleep already?" (Sometimes Ansley teaches English at school.) I have slept in her hut on many nights, and just as I begin to ask her all the world's most important questions, she's gone. Ugh. Sometimes she apologizes before she drops off, but she drops off nonetheless.

Dinga moved back to the house of her real mother last week, but she just can't seem to stay away from ours. She came in late—probably after everyone had fallen asleep at her own house—and joined us for the night, weaving her little body in between Pabris's and mine. Then Tony came in at a right angle to share Jolie's pillow with me. I woke during the night and found that his side of the pillow was soaking wet. I still don't understand how it got soaked, but I can speculate. Oh, and he had found a way to somehow get my covers again too—so I had a little edge while he ended up with the big square nicely covering all of his body.

I think I was made for this style of sleeping—
love it!
I hate sleeping by myself—
hate it!
It's always been that way.

I can feel Dinga's arrhythmic heart to one side of me and Armelle's deep breathing in my ear and Tony unconsciously fighting me for space on the pillow. I feel like the night is another day. I'll often wake up so many times and have so many short conversations with those sleeping close to me that it feels like I am getting to know people better all night long! I have only three more nights. I'll miss this horribly.

Holy Spirit light

These connections are a blessing that I have found and that I'm hoping I'll keep forever. I read somewhere that this connection between people is God working to weave us together. I've felt that. He is the link, and He is the flow between.

Sometimes I worry, though. The manifestations of God that I've seen here are very touchable and seeable and hearable. And I feel like that over-used phrase—empty but filled. I worry that this gold mine is forever in Chad, among this family here, and that when I leave, I'm leaving it in this village, under these grass roofs.

However, I've felt encouraged lately too. I've thought about how we feel hunger every day. It's one of the constants that we anticipate and plan for—like the tide or the four seasons of the Northwest. I relate to the Israelites, who were aware of and tired of their hunger for food. God sent them manna daily to satisfy this basic need—and when the Israelites had the manna, they worried that they wouldn't have it the next day, so they stored more than they needed that day. But the stored manna spoiled before the next day. So the Israelites had to trust daily that they would have what they needed.

And I've felt God saying, "Trust that you don't have to cling to My presence here. Trust that I always am everywhere you are and will continue to reveal Myself in ways that only I can. Trust that I've given this light that you're seeing now for the moment you need it, and that the Holy Spirit light will continue to be with you wherever you go."

wind and rain

I feel like you must think that all I do is lie on mats and sleep these days, because that's all I write about. But yet again, I must tell you one of these stories. Last night we were lying on mats and cots and bedsprings and blankets, and the sea of people was quiet except for Jolie's melodic singing. As she gets sleepier, her singing turns into mumbling in notes and the volume fades. The only other noises come from Tony and Izeedoor, who are talking mathematics by lamplight, and from Armelle, who cries once in a while for silly spoiled reasons.

Oh, and then there is the hum of the wind—that emotional wind. I'm not sure exactly what the emotions are as it whips around our covers. Anger? Love? Confidence? Determination?

Oh, and those trees.

Oh, and my thoughts. It's rare that wind doesn't make us think. And we let the brain go a lot of the time. "Sure, brain, we can go there." I can think of a hundred things in ten minutes. Really, it can happen. One bounce to another bounce to another, and I'm all over the issues and joys of life.

The wind blew dust in my eyes, and the blossoms it blew off the tree got stuck in my hair. And as the tree above me loomed and rustled and swayed, I kept thinking about how bad it would hurt to have a branch fall on me.

Esther woke up, and we talked about rain. I told her I had really wished I had been here for more of the rainy season, and how fun it would be if it rained just once more. But Esther said very certainly, "Emilio, it's not going to rain. This is the driest time of the year. This is just wind."

Jolie woke up, too, and she went to make tea. Then we drank tea while on our cots, which were parallel and about two inches apart. Jolie lay on her side and me on my stomach as we chatted. She's such a graceful, life-filled lady. Armelle climbed up and found a niche against Jolie's body.

After we finished our tea, we stopped talking, and I turned onto my back. Maybe it was the way the branches shook themselves at me and the way the stars were fading in and out of the clouds—appearing and disappearing. Maybe it was the anticipation of the dust and flowers landing in my eyes. Whatever it was, I was melancholic and attentive to my thoughts, which were focused on the future: what's next for me?

Most of my "what's next" thinking is about school, goals, relationships, and similar things: What do I do now with my life and na-na-na, blah, blah, blah? And while my mind was distracted, drops of water started making my eyes blink and my body flinch, and the scent in the air changed to *rain*! Esther ate her words, and I rubbed it in! She smiled and made some comment about how it would stop soon, about it not being normal.

But it got me thinking. When will *what's next* actually be *what I expect?* It doesn't happen often. It never rains until May; it's the driest part of the year right now—but it rained. It rained in the dry season, and that—knowing that probability and uncertainty are uncertain themselves—let me trust more. What seems to be or should be might not be because life is miraculous and spontaneous, yet guided through the turns!

Thoughts.

Thoughts.

Thoughts.

But something outside of my mind seems to sit calmly beside my overactive brain and says, *"Be still and know that I am God."* Who is it? Where's it coming from? And I want more from that subtle Voice! After all, we are productive people, and we could be multiplying fractions and doing long division and solving the problem of food shortages.

Be still and know one thing?

So hard. *Knowing* that one thing can be tricky as it is, and it probably requires all of our attention. Yes, that's probably it.

Be still and know.

goodbyes

We make sure to say heartfelt goodbyes to those whom we couldn't imagine never having said Hello to. I always tell myself that I'm going to be prepared to leave a place. I make lists of everything important to do, every loose end to tie up, every gift to give, and every person to connect to one last time. But every time I find myself unprepared for the splitting, running around trying to have that nice, warm feeling, but instead have feelings of dissatisfaction and frustration that seem to edge out my happy sentiments and leave me feeling anxious.

This time I felt a combination of feelings: relief to be leaving, guilt for abandoning people I cared about, heart-soreness because of the kind words said at parting, uncertainty about what lies ahead, yet also assurance that life still has the qualities of surprise and progress that I so love, and that *this* departure also carried those qualities and wouldn't let me down—I would be surprised when I went around the next bend. And the next. And the next.

But the attractions of the next bend don't make getting on the road easier. I still had to hug my African mother goodbye, kiss my little Armelle, and make promises to see my sister Dinga again soon—all the while knowing that for those whom I left behind, life was never guaranteed.

The feeling of relief came from the fact that I felt like I had made it to a gas station after running on empty for a lengthy stretch of highway. You always think you know how far you can go on empty, but you never know for sure. There were times when I felt like I wasn't strong enough to bear the tension, and it was a relief to be leaving with my spirit intact.

I felt a bit like a bad person when I realized that those who were remaining at the hospital would be continuing to face the very moments of intense stress and frustration that I was relieving my heart of by leaving. Even now, when the clock ticks five o'clock, I know the patients are getting their bleach-water dressing changes, and at midnight I think of an overworked nurse giving that painful penicillin IV in the isolation ward. I imagine that tonight the babies with meningitis won't stop crying, and whichever nurse is guarding their beds will feel fingernails scraping against the chalkboards of his or her insides. The helplessness is often painful.

I felt guilt as I walked through the hospital for the last time. I saw a girl, whose burns were lying open to the air yet shielded from the merciless insects by a thin mosquito net, cry out in pain. I saw a baby's whole sack-of-bones self cry out for milk. I saw my friend Caroline, a nurse from California, plead with a family to buy the medicine their baby needed. And as I was walking out of the pediatrics ward, a man tapped my arm and said, "My child's IV has stopped. Can you fix it?"

Caroline came over quickly and said, "I'll take care of that; she's not working right now." It's true. I'd come to the end of my work in Béré Hospital, and something about that fact left a little guilty bite on me.

My heart ached at the kind words people spoke to me at my parting. Jolie's embrace and four simple sobs followed by the shaking of her upward-facing, outstretched palms—a motion that said our parting was leaving something lacking—warmed me and hurt me at the same time.

Mounden asked me, "What will I do when you leave, Emily? Who is going to give me money to buy pigeons?" and then he laughed. He spoke his last words to me as I sat on the public transport. "Emily," he said, directing his comment through the slider window frame, "it is God who is going to guard your heart."

What he said was so true that I wanted to jump back out of the van, grab him by his shoulders, and tell him he knew something really important; that those weren't just words, and that indeed God will guard our hearts—the inflow and outflow of them. Our hearts are shaped and taught by the hard things we endure, and then filled and enlarged by the little and big bursts of happiness we experience.

But, for the moment, our time for meaningful conversation had passed. I continued waving my hand out the window of that ridiculously packed van long after I couldn't crane my neck in their direction anymore.

In an e-mail a good friend of mine sent to me soon after leaving, that friend wrote, "The reason we sometimes hate to leave is that we fear we will forget the things we have experienced." Right now the time I spent in Béré, Chad, Africa, is deeply meaningful and intensely real to me, but we all know that as we slip back into our "normal" lives, the details of an experience can start whispering instead of screaming their significance. However, though we may forget the experience and even the lessons learned, our hearts have been changed forever. Forever.

And the strength we find in hearts that have grown larger and stronger makes all the cutting and tapping and pounding and boiling worth it. And the movement inside our chest and bursting out of our ribs is life. It's our heart beating in rhythm, with rhymes and poems and stories and songs.

God up there, let our hearts swell bigger every day.

touchdown home

I'm on my way home, fog just flying by the smudged plastic window—smudged by the curious awe of children, by their noses pressed and eyes peering. Spokane, my home since birth, is unveiled quickly and increased in size. I've been paraded over America as if to say, "Here is where your feet will touch next, Emily. Take a good look, because when we touch down, you'll be right in the pressure of it all." And sure enough, the closer the ground got, the faster it flew by, and everything shook when we touched down.

Epilogue

In October of 2010, I returned to work at the hospital in Béré, and I spent another two months with Samedi and Jolie and their family. Late one night during that second stint, Jolie, Samedi, and I were reminiscing about my first six months with them. Knowing the language better by that time, I was able to tell them how I had felt my first evening in Béré, my first evening in with them. This is what I had written in my journal.

> It's my first real evening in my new home and I'm crying already. I'm not much of a crier usually. But tonight, I can't plug my eyes. As dusk settled in, they put me in my dark mud hut to eat—alone. Supposedly, it's a real honor to get to eat like this, to have your own bowl of food and not be "disturbed" by that joyous noise of happy children. They definitely don't know me yet.

I said to them, "I was CRYING in my hut that night! You put me in there alone!"

Samedi sweetly said, "Really?"

I said, "Yes!"

Jolie grabbed my hand and said, "Aye, Emily! You cried?"

Then Samedi said thoughtfully, "Emily, we had never had a white person live with us before—we didn't know if you would eat with us. It was all so new for us too. We learned that you wanted to eat with us, and we stopped putting you in your hut alone."

Some people have wondered what good a twenty-two-year-old can do at a hospital in the desert, and if we're talking saving lives or saving the world, those people are right on—I certainly didn't save any worlds. But the deep learning that makes you do something differently for people the next time you're with them because you understand who they are and how they think and how they do things—it's that kind of learning that changes the world.

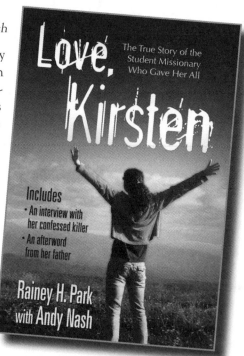